500 RECIPES
COOKING THE CHINESE WAY

by Nina Froud

HAMLYN

LONDON · NEW YORK · SYDNEY · TORONTO

Published by
The Hamlyn Publishing Group Limited
London · New York · Sydney · Toronto
Astronaut House, Feltham, Middlesex, England

© Copyright The Hamlyn Publishing Group Limited 1960
ISBN 0 600 03432 1

First published 1960
Eighth impression 1975

Printed in England by Index Printers, Dunstable, Bedfordshire

Contents

Introduction

Chinese cookery, like Chinese art and literature, has a distinct personality of its own. There really is nothing like it. The tremendous variety in the cooking admirably reflects the taste and talent of the Chinese people who have always been discerning and fastidious about their food. It is recorded in the Analects that Confucius – as far back as twenty-five centuries ago – spoke against eating 'anything over-cooked, under-cooked, crookedly cut or deficient in seasoning'.

Chinese intellectuals never thought it beneath their dignity to concern themselves with food and the 12th century poet Su Tung Po produced many poetical recipes, the most quoted of which says:

> Lack of bamboo makes one vulgar,
> Lack of pork makes one thin,
> To avoid being vulgar and skinny,
> Treat yourself to pork with bamboo shoots.

Chinese delicacies are innumerable. Every province of that vast country has contributed a great number of dishes to the national repertoire, but in this book I shall confine myself mainly to the Canton cuisine, because the best – gastronomically speaking – years of my life were spent in South China and because it is indisputably the greatest of them all.

Chinese culinary methods differ from the European chiefly by the fact that *boiling* as such is practically never resorted to. Food is stewed, braised, semi-fried, deep-fried, roasted – both meat and vegetables are often 'scrambled' – but, with the exception of rice, never, never just plain boiled.

There are other fundamental differences. For instance, in England (and elsewhere in Europe) the guest is expected to do his own cutting; in China all his food is cut up for him in the kitchen and such savage implements as knives never figure on the dinner table.

In England it is usually left to the eater to season his food. The Chinese, like the French, consider this an essential part of the cook's job and seasoning and condiments are used to develop the inherent flavour of the ingredients, to produce the important chemical reaction between the food and the seasoning under the influence of heat.

The Chinese eat their food with chopsticks, which is the best way to eat Chinese food. I have often felt sorry for Europeans spooning some delicate morsel drowned in too much sauce. The chopsticks enable one to hold just as much sauce as coats the morsel, which is the correct proportion, if all the subtle interchanges of flavour are to be enjoyed. Contrary to all rumours, chopsticks are not difficult to manipulate and the difference their use makes to the enjoyment of Chinese food is tremendous.

And finally, no desserts or sweets are normally served at ordinary home or restaurant meals, which is probably the reason why the Chinese usually look twenty years younger than their age, keep their teeth and the women preserve their 'line' long past middle age.

Some Useful Facts and Figures

Comparison of Weights and Measures

English weights and measures have been used throughout the book. 3 teaspoonfuls equal 1 tablespoon. The average English teacup is ¼ pint. The average English breakfast cup is ½ pint. When cups are mentioned in recipes they refer to a B.S.I. measuring cup which holds ½ pint or 10 fluid ounces. In case it is wished to translate quantities into American or metric counterparts the following give a comparison.

Liquid measure

The American pint is 16 fluid ounces, as opposed to the British Imperial pint and Canadian pint which are 20 fluid ounces. The American ½-pint measuring cup is therefore equivalent to ⅖ British pint. In Australia the British Imperial pint, 20 fluid ounces, is used.

Solid measure

British	American
1 lb. butter or other fat	2 cups
1 lb. flour	4 cups
1 lb. granulated or castor sugar	2 cups
1 lb. icing or confectioners' sugar	3½ cups
1 lb brown sugar (firmly packed)	2 cups
12 oz. golden syrup or treacle	1 cup
14 oz. rice	2 cups
1 lb. dried fruit	3 cups
1 lb. chopped or minced meat (firmly packed)	2 cups
1 lb. lentils or split peas	2 cups
2 oz. soft breadcrumbs	1 cup
½ oz. flour	2 tablespoons
1 oz. flour	¼ cup
1 oz. sugar	2 tablespoons
½ oz. butter	1 tablespoon
1 oz. golden syrup or treacle	1 tablespoon
1 oz. jam or jelly	1 tablespoon

All U.S. standard measuring cups and spoons

To help you understand metrication

You will see from the chart that 1 oz. is approximately 28 g. but can be rounded off to the more convenient measuring unit of 25. Also the figures in the right hand column are not always increased by 25. This is to reduce the difference between the convenient number and the nearest equivalent. If in a recipe the ingredients to be converted are 1 oz. of margarine and 6 oz. of flour, these are the conversions: 25 g. margarine and 175 g. flour.

The conversion chart

Ounces	Approx. g. and ml. to nearest whole number	Approx. to nearest unit of 25
1	28	25
2	57	50
3	85	75
4	113	125
5	142	150
6	170	175
7	198	200
8	226	225
12	340	350
16	456	450

Note: When converting quantities over 16 oz. first add the appropriate figures in the centre column, not those given in the right hand column, THEN adjust to the nearest unit of 25g. For example, to convert 1¾ lb. add 456 g. to 340 g. which equals 796 g. When rounded off to the convenient figure it becomes 800 g.

Approximate liquid conversions

¼ pint–150 ml.   1,000 millilitres–1 l (litre)
½ pint–275 ml.   1 l–1¾ pints
¾ pint–425 ml.   ½ l–¾ pint plus 4 tablespoons
1 pint–575 ml.   1 dl. (decilitre)–6 tablespoons

Note: If solid ingredients give scant weight using the 25 unit conversion, the amount of liquid allowed must also be scant. For example, although 575 ml. is nearer to 1 pint (20 fluid oz.) when making a white pouring sauce use 550 ml. of milk to 25 g. each of butter and flour for a better consistency.

Oven Temperatures

The following chart gives conversions from degrees Fahrenheit to degrees Celsius (formerly known as Centigrade). This chart is accurate to within 3° Celsius, and can therefore be used for recipes which give oven temperatures in metric.

Description	Electric Setting	Gas Mark
very cool	225°F–110°C	$\frac{1}{4}$
	250°F–130°C	$\frac{1}{2}$
cool	275°F–140°C	1
	300°F–150°C	2
moderate	325°F–170°C	3
	350°F–180°C	4
moderately	375°F–190°C	5
hot	400°F–200°C	6
hot	425°F–220°C	7
	450°F–230°C	8
very hot	475°F–240°C	9

Note: This table is an approximate guide only. Different makes of cooker vary and if you are in any doubt about the setting it is as well to refer to the manufacturer's temperature chart.

General Remarks

People who like Chinese food and are competent cooks often hesitate to take on the preparation of a Chinese meal, because they have an almost superstitious fear that it must take 'weeks to prepare'.

There are, of course, in Chinese (as in French) cuisine special gala dishes which require several days' preparation, but the normal, everyday Chinese cooking is a very far cry indeed from the complicated ordeal which people erroneously believe it to be. True, the cutting and the other preliminary preparations take some time, but the actual cooking of most of the dishes is literally a matter of a few minutes.

Ordinary kitchen equipment is perfectly adaptable for Chinese cooking.

There are a few basic Chinese ingredients which are essential. Among the indispensables I would put Soya bean sauce (it is not cheap but a bottle lasts a long time) and green ginger. Chinese mixed pickles, Oyster Sauce, Ve-Tsin, Bamboo . Shoots, Peanut oil, dried mushrooms, Water Chestnuts, and 'Mien' – dried noodles – are all easily obtainable.

Chinese food must be served immediately it is turned out of the frying pan. The order of serving at a formal function is first cold dishes, then fried dishes, followed by braised and stewed dishes with rice. In a Chinese home, however, five or six dishes (often comprising rice or noodles, a meat dish, a fish dish, a soup and a vegetable dish) would be served all at once.

It has of late become more and more the fashion to serve wine with Chinese food, but it is an artificially fostered 'foreign' custom. However, even if you fall from grace and drink wine with your meal, let the civilizing, mellowing action of the food have its effect and, at the end of the meal, switch to China tea – the fragrant, national beverage which alone makes a fitting end to a Chinese meal. The most exciting thing about Chinese cookery is the scope it gives one's imagina-tion. Provided one concentrates faithfully on the bringing together of subtle flavours – the sky's the limit.

It is impossible to write a book on Chinese cookery without mentioning 'Chop Suey', the dish which so prominently figures on menus of Chinese restaurants outside China. The words roughly mean something like 'a mixture of chopped up bits and pieces' and the dish is neither known nor eaten in China.

Chinese Flavourings and Ingredients

Soya Sauce (also called soya bean sauce, or just plain soya) is made from pulped soya beans. There are two kinds, the light coloured one used mainly for cooking and the dark coloured one for the table.

Ve-Tsin – the basis of which is monosodium glutamate, subtly brings out the natural flavour of other ingredients, but must be used extremely sparingly. The European and American equivalent is Accent.

Oyster Sauce – which as its name indicates is made from oysters. It has the ability to blend with and intensify the flavour of a dish.

All these, along with **Thick Sweet Sauce** and **Spicery Salt,** are used undiluted.

Cornflour – is used mainly for thickening soups and sauces and less frequently as a sub-stitute for flour when dredging ingredients before deep frying. 1 teaspoon of cornflour mixed with 2 tablespoons of cold water makes a thin paste which is then added to the soup or sauce.

Star Aniseed, Chinese Pickles, Chinese Pickled Onions, Lotus Seeds – both fresh and preserved – **Green Ginger, Bamboo Shoots, Water Chestnuts** and **Bean Curd** are used as they stand and require no preliminary prepa-ration except where specified in individual recipes. Others like the dried vegetables need soaking in water before cooking.

Dried Mushrooms – soak in water for 1 hour, then remove stalks. In various stewed dishes, the soaking time is reduced, this is indicated in specific recipes.

Lichen – soak for 15 minutes in hot water.

Lily Petals – soak for 15 minutes in hot water.

Preserved Parsnips – soak for 10 minutes in hot water.

Lotus Roots – soak for 20 minutes in hot water.

Bark Gwor (white nuts) – remove shell, break open the kernel, and take out the small root inside. Soak this for 2 hours in cold water.

Soups

Soups form an essential part of the Chinese menu, whether the meal is a banquet in a restaurant or a modest home dinner. In restaurants it is sometimes served in individual bowls but in China it is customary to serve soup in one large bowl from which it is ladled into individual guests' bowls.

Generally speaking, Chinese soups are clear and light as opposed to thick and heavy, this is why traditionally they are served between courses or at the end of the meal to freshen the palate.

Chinese stock

Whenever possible, Chinese primary stock should be used instead of water to ensure the success of a dish. Usually, the stock is made of equal quantities of chicken and lean pork, allowing 8 oz. of each to a pint of water. Proceed as follows: Cut the meat into small pieces, weigh it and put into a large saucepan with water in proportion. Bring to the boil, then simmer slowly until the liquid is reduced by half. Strain through a cloth and remove all traces of fat. Keep in a cool place and use as required.

Certain recipes call for veal or chicken stock, and this can be made either of veal or chicken or a mixture of both in equal proportions, prepared as described above.

Sweet corn soup with pork

cooking time   55 minutes

you will need for 4–6 servings:

1 lb. lean pork or 8 oz. chicken giblets (keep 2–3 slices finely shredded for garnish)	¼ teaspoon Ve-Tsin cornflour (for dredging) 1 egg, well-beaten salt
2 pints water	little ham, finely shredded, (optional)
1 small knob ginger	
1 can sweet corn	1 teaspoon cornflour (for thickening)
1 teaspoon brandy (or dry sherry)	2 tablespoons cold water

1 Cut the remainder of pork into small pieces and put into a pan with water and ginger.
2 Bring to the boil, simmer for 45 minutes, then add sweet corn, brandy and Ve-Tsin.
3 Simmer for 5 minutes.
4 Add a small quantity of finely shredded pork dredged with dry cornflour. Cook 5 minutes.
5 Add egg, stir, season to taste.
6 Garnish with ham and chicken. Thicken with cornflour and water.

Sweet corn soup with chicken

cooking time   40 minutes

you will need for 4–6 servings:

8 oz. breast of chicken (keep 1–2 slices, finely shredded for garnish)	cornflour (for dredging) 1 egg, well-beaten salt
1 small knob ginger	little ham, finely shredded
1 can sweet corn	
¼ teaspoon Ve-Tsin	1 teaspoon cornflour (for thickening)
1 teaspoon brandy (or dry sherry)	2 tablespoons cold water

1 Slice half the chicken finely and bring to the boil in the water together with the bones and ginger.
2 Simmer for 30 minutes, then add sweet corn, Ve-Tsin and brandy.
3 Simmer for 5 minutes, add rest of chicken finely shredded and dredged with dry cornflour.
4 Add egg, stir, season to taste.
5 Garnish with ham and chicken, and thicken with cornflour and water.

Prawn soup

cooking time   40 minutes

you will need for 4–6 servings:

12 oz. raw prawns, peeled	salt
4 oz. rice	1 small lettuce, shredded
cold water	

1 Chop the prawns.
2 Wash rice and boil in water.
3 Simmer until rice softens and makes a thick soup, then add prawns and salt to taste.
4 Simmer for 10 minutes.
5 Sprinkle with lettuce and serve.

Asparagus soup

cooking time   30–45 minutes

you will need for 4–6 servings:

8 oz. breast of chicken	1 teaspoon brandy (or dry sherry)
2 pints water	
1 can asparagus tips (or 1 small bundle fresh asparagus)	1 teaspoon cornflour 2 tablespoons cold water salt
¼ teaspoon Ve-Tsin	knob green ginger (optional)

1 Slice the chicken and boil in water with the asparagus and its liquid.
2 Simmer for 30 minutes.
3 Add Ve-Tsin and brandy.
4 Thicken with cornflour and water.
5 Salt to taste and serve.

Note:

When fresh asparagus is used it should be cut into slices 1-inch long and boiled uncovered with the ginger and the chicken for 45 minutes.

Egg and pea soup

cooking time   30 minutes

you will need for 4–6 servings:

8 oz. lean pork (or 8 oz. chicken)	¼ teaspoon Ve-Tsin 1 teaspoon brandy (or dry sherry)
2½ pints water	
8 oz. young green peas	2 eggs, well-beaten
small knob green ginger	salt

1 Slice the pork, bring to boil in water with peas and ginger.
2 Simmer for 30 minutes, add Ve-Tsin, brandy and eggs.
3 Bring to the boil, salt to taste and serve at once.

Plain egg soup

cooking time   10–15 minutes

you will need for 4–6 servings:

¼ teaspoon peanut oil	small bunch spring onions, chopped
2 pints water	
4 oz. pork	1 dessertspoon light soya sauce
1 teaspoon salt	
2 eggs, well-beaten	

1 Heat oil in saucepan and when hot add water and bring to boil.
2 Shred pork into short strips and add to water.
3 Add salt, simmer for 5 minutes and remove pan from heat.
4 Add eggs, sprinkle with spring onions, season with soya sauce, and serve at once.

Lettuce and egg soup

cooking time   35–40 minutes

you will need for 4–6 servings:

8 oz. lean pork	1 teaspoon brandy
1 small lettuce	(or dry sherry)
small knob green ginger	2 eggs, well-beaten
2½ pints water	salt
¼ teaspoon Ve-Tsin	

1 Cut pork into thin slices and shred lettuce.
2 Boil pork and ginger in water for 30 minutes.
3 Add Ve-Tsin, brandy and lettuce.
4 Boil fast for 5 minutes with the lid off, add eggs, salt to taste and serve.

Lettuce and shrimp soup

cooking time   15 minutes

you will need for 4–6 servings:

1 small lettuce	1 teaspoon salt
4 oz. pork	1 dessertspoon light
2 pints water	soya sauce
1 tablespoon dried shrimps	

1 Shred lettuce and pork finely.
2 Bring water to boil and add pork, shrimps and salt, and simmer gently for 10 minutes.
3 Add lettuce and cook for 1 minute.
4 Add soya sauce and serve.

Cabbage soup

cooking time   10–12 minutes

you will need for 4–6 servings:

3 heads Chinese cabbage	1 teaspoon salt
(or Savoy cabbage)	1 dessertspoon light
4 oz. pork	soya sauce
2½ pints water	

1 Wash and cut cabbage into small pieces, rejecting all coarse parts.
2 Slice pork into fine shreds.
3 Bring water to boil, add salt and pork.
4 Simmer for 5 minutes, add cabbage and soya sauce and simmer for further 2 minutes, keeping the pan uncovered to prevent cabbage losing its colour.
5 Serve at once.

Shrimp and cabbage soup

cooking time   15 minutes

you will need for 4 servings:

8 oz. fresh shrimps	1 teaspoon salt
2 egg whites, beaten stiff	2–2½ pints boiling water
2 slices ginger, pounded	2 tablespoons cornflour
8 oz. cabbage, shredded	3 tablespoons cold water
4 oz. celery, shredded	1–2 spring onions, chopped

1 Shell, rinse and drain shrimps.
2 Chop finely and mix with egg whites and ginger.
3 Cook cabbage and celery in salted water for 8 minutes.
4 Mix cornflour with water, and blend into cooked vegetables.
5 Bring to the boil, cook for 2 minutes, stirring all the time.
6 Add shrimps, bring to boil, simmer for 5 minutes, add spring onions and serve.

Celery cabbage soup

cooking time   3 minutes

you will need for 4–6 servings:

2 tablespoons cooking oil	8 oz. celery cabbage
1 tablespoon soya sauce	(or cos lettuce or
1 teaspoon salt	celeriac) finely chopped
½ teaspoon pepper	few drops sesame oil
8 oz. beef, finely chopped	2–3 spring onions, chopped
2½–3 pints stock (or water)	

1 Mix the oil, soya sauce, salt and pepper.
2 Spread this mixture over the beef and leave in a cool place for 1–2 hours.
3 Bring the stock to boil, add celery cabbage. Cook for 1 minute.
4 Add sesame oil and beef. Bring to the boil again, add spring onions and serve.

Water melon soup

cooking time   2 hours 10 minutes

you will need for 4–6 servings:

1 oz. dried mushrooms	8 oz. raw chicken, shredded
4 oz. bamboo shoots,	8 oz. pork, shredded
4 oz. lean ham (or bacon)	¼ teaspoon Ve-Tsin
1 water melon (4–5 lb.)	1 knob green ginger

1 Blanch mushrooms and cut into thin strips.
2 Dice the bamboo shoots and cut ham in shreds.
3 Cut top off melon and remove some pulp and seeds to enlarge the cavity.
4 Boil chicken, pork, Ve-Tsin, ginger, mushrooms and bamboo shoots, together with any bones, then simmer gently for 40 minutes.
5 Remove all bones from soup, add ham, and pour the whole inside the melon, replacing the top.
6 Place the melon in a large pudding basin to keep it upright and steam for 1½ hours or until melon is completely cooked. Serve whole.
Note:
The melon is placed on the table, and as melon and soup are scooped out the melon peel is cut down to the required level. If more soup is needed it can be heated and added to the melon.

9

Mushroom soup

cooking time   1 hour

you will need for 4—6 servings:

4 oz. dried mushrooms (or 8 oz. fresh mushrooms)	¼ teaspoon Ve-Tsin
	2½—3 pints water
1 lb. meat (pork, giblets, chicken or beef)	salt
	green ginger (optional)
	egg, beaten (optional)

1 Blanch the dried mushrooms and soak in hot water until soft. (Fresh mushrooms do not need any preliminary treatment.)
2 Cut meat into slices and bring to the boil with the mushrooms.
3 Add Ve-Tsin and simmer for 1 hour. Salt to taste and serve.

Note:

If fresh mushrooms are used, green ginger is boiled with the meat and the mushrooms are added 20 minutes before serving. Egg can be added to the soup just before serving.

Mushroom and green pea soup

cooking time   15—17 minutes

you will need for 4—6 servings:

6 small, dried Chinese mushrooms	2½ pints water
	1 teaspoon salt
8 oz. fresh garden peas	1 dessertspoon light soya sauce
4 oz. pork	

1 Soak mushrooms in warm water until soft, then dice.
2 Shell peas and cut pork into thin strips.
3 Bring water to the boil, add mushrooms and salt.
4 Simmer for 10 minutes, add pork and peas, and cook with the lid off until peas are done.
5 Add soya sauce and serve at once.

Abalone and green pea soup

cooking time   10—12 minutes

you will need for 4—6 servings:

4 dried mushrooms	1 teaspoon salt
1 small can abalone	2 pints water
8 oz. fresh garden peas	1 dessertspoon light soya sauce
4 oz. pork	

1 Soak mushrooms in warm water until soft; dice mushrooms and abalone, keeping the abalone juice.
2 Shell peas and cut pork into thin strips.
3 Salt the water, bring to boil and simmer mushrooms and pork in it for 5 minutes.
4 Add peas and cook until tender.
5 Add abalone, abalone juice and soya sauce, bring to the boil and serve.

Abalone and pork soup

cooking time   4—5 minutes

you will need for 6 servings:

6 oz. lean pork	1 teaspoon Chinese wine (or sherry)
2 teaspoons cornflour	
1½ tablespoons soya sauce	salt
	½ can abalone
	2½ pints water

1 Cut pork into thin slices. Sprinkle with cornflour, soya sauce, wine and a pinch of salt. Mix well.
2 Strain abalone, keeping all the juice. Cut into very thin slices.
3 Bring water to the boil, add abalone juice. As soon as boiling is re-established, add pork.
4 Taste liquid for seasoning; if necessary, add more salt. Bring to the boil.
5 Add abalone, cook for 2 minutes and serve.

Mixed vegetable soup

cooking time   20 minutes

you will need for 4 servings:

8 oz. fresh mushrooms	4 oz. spring greens
2 tablespoons sesame oil (or olive oil)	small bunch watercress
	2 pints boiling water
8 oz. spinach	salt and pepper

1 Prepare mushroom oil by cutting the mushrooms into fine slices and frying in hot oil on a very low heat for 5 minutes.
2 Wash and clean the vegetables, cut into pieces and sauté in half the mushroom oil, keeping the rest for future use.
3 Cook gently for 5 minutes, then add water and simmer for 10 minutes.
4 Season with salt and pepper and serve.

Bean sprout soup

cooking time   13 minutes

you will need for 4—6 servings:

8 oz. bean sprouts	1 dessertspoon light soya sauce
4 oz. pork	
2—2½ pints water	few spring onions, chopped
1 teaspoon salt	

1 Wash and drain bean sprouts.
2 Cut pork into thin slices.
3 Bring water to boil and add pork seasoned with salt, simmer for 5 minutes.
4 Add bean sprouts and simmer for a further 8 minutes.
5 Add soya sauce, sprinkle with spring onions and serve.

Spinach soup

cooking time   12 minutes

you will need for 4–6 servings:

2 lb. fresh spinach (or 1 large packet frozen spinach)	2 pints hot water
	1 teaspoon salt
4 oz. pork	1 dessertspoon light soya sauce

1 Pick over spinach, wash and cut into small pieces.
2 Cut pork finely.
3 Bring water to boil and add pork and salt.
4 Simmer gently for 5 minutes. Add spinach and cook for 6–7 minutes. Serve with soya sauce.

Tomato and egg soup

cooking time   5–6 minutes

you will need for 4–6 servings:

2½–3 pints stock	1 teaspoon sugar
8 oz. tomatoes, chopped and peeled	1 teaspoon salt
	¼ teaspoon pepper
2 tablespoons cornflour	2 eggs, well-beaten
2 tablespoons cold water	

1 Bring stock to the boil, add tomatoes, cover and simmer for 3 minutes.
2 Make a paste of cornflour, water, sugar, salt and pepper and add to stock.
3 Stir until smooth, reduce heat, add eggs.
4 Cook, stirring for one minute until the eggs form shreds, then serve.

Watercress soup

cooking time   7–8 minutes

you will need for 4–6 servings:

1 bunch watercress	2 pieces dried tangerine peel
2½ pints water	
8 oz. lean beef, finely shredded	1 teaspoon salt
2 slices green ginger	1 dessertspoon light soya sauce

1 Clean and cut watercress into 1¼-inch lengths.
2 Bring water to boil and add all ingredients.
3 Cook for 7–8 minutes, then serve.

Birds' nest soup

cooking time   2 hours 15 minutes

you will need for 6–8 servings:

4 oz. birds' nest	2 oz. cooked chicken, chopped
2 pints chicken stock	
1 leg of chicken	1 oz. ham, finely chopped
2 teaspoons water chestnut flour	2 oz. fresh mushrooms, chopped
water	few spring onions, chopped
salt and pepper	
1 egg white	

1 Soak the birds' nest in hot water for 4 hours.
2 Simmer in chicken stock for 10 minutes.
3 Transfer to fireproof dish, place chicken leg on top and steam for 2 hours.
4 Remove chicken leg and any water that may have dropped on the birds' nest.
5 Mix water chestnut flour with water to a smooth paste.
6 Place birds' nest in saucepan, cover with stock, bring to boil, season with salt and pepper and stir in water chestnut paste.
7 Simmer for 2 minutes, stirring all the time.
8 Add white of egg, and when soup becomes semi-transparent, garnish with chicken, ham, mushrooms and spring onions. Serve.

Birds' nest in whole chicken

cooking time   2 hours 35 minutes

you will need for 6–8 servings:

2 oz. birds' nest	3 teaspoons gin
water	2½ pints chicken stock
1 chicken leg	
1 young chicken (4–5 lb.)	

1 Soak the birds' nest in hot water for 4 hours.
2 Put it in a saucepan, cover with water and boil for 5 minutes.
3 Transfer into ovenproof dish, place on top chicken leg and steam for 2¼ hours.
4 Clean the chicken, open at the neck and take out inside and all bones, taking care not to break the skin.
5 Pour gin inside chicken and shake well.
6 Stuff chicken with birds' nest, moisten with enough stock to fill chicken. Sew up neck opening.
7 Place chicken in basin, pour in enough stock to cover and steam for 1 hour. Remove 'stitches' before serving.

Soup with chicken and fried noodles

cooking time   5 minutes

you will need for 4–6 servings:

6 oz. breast of chicken	hot chicken stock
1 oz. mushrooms	salt and pepper
1 oz. bamboo shoots	little sesame oil
1 round fried noodles	1 oz. spring onions, chopped
boiling water	

1 Slice chicken, mushrooms and bamboo shoots finely.
2 Place noodles in pan of boiling water for 2 minutes, then drain and put in serving bowl.
3 Place chicken, mushrooms and bamboo shoots in a pan.
4 Add double the amount of stock required to cover the ingredients, and cook for 3 minutes.
5 Add salt and pepper to taste and pour over the noodles.
6 Sprinkle with a few drops of sesame oil and the spring onions and serve.

Chicken soup with egg

cooking time   2–3 minutes

you will need for 4–6 servings:

2½–3 tablespoons cornflour	¼ teaspoon pepper
2½–3 tablespoons cold water	2½–3 pints hot chicken stock
½ teaspoon sugar	2 eggs, beaten
1 teaspoon salt	2–3 spring onions, chopped

1 Make a smooth paste of cornflour and water, sugar, salt and pepper.
2 Pour into the stock and stir.
3 Bring to the boil, reduce heat, add eggs, stir for 1 minute, until the eggs go into shreds.
4 Remove from heat, garnish with spring onions and serve.

Chicken soup with egg dice and rice

cooking time   5 minutes

you will need for 4–6 servings:

2½–3 pints chicken stock	¼ teaspoon pepper
2 eggs	2 spring onions, chopped
½ teaspoon sugar	1 tablespoon oil
1 teaspoon salt	8 oz. cooked rice

1 Heat the stock.
2 Beat eggs with sugar, salt, pepper and onions.
3 Fry this mixture in oil as an omelette, turning it to cook both sides. Allow to cool, cut into small dice.
4 Put rice into boiling stock to heat through, stir, add seasoning if necessary.
5 Pour into bowls, garnish with egg dice and serve.

Variation

Chicken soup with egg dice

As above, omitting the rice. At the last moment, just before adding egg dice, stir in a little soya sauce to taste.

Chicken and ham soup

cooking time   2½–3 hours

you will need for 6–8 servings:

1 boiling fowl, cleaned	4 oz. Chinese ham, shredded
4 pints water	few spring onions, chopped
2 oz. awabi, dried	
2 tablespoons sherry	
2 teaspoons salt	

1 Put chicken in water and bring to the boil.
2 Add awabi, sherry, salt and ham.
3 Simmer gently for 2½–3 hours. Before serving, sprinkle with spring onions.

Note:

If awabi is not available, prawns can be substituted.

Chicken and mushroom soup

cooking time   8–10 minutes

you will need for 6 servings:

2 oz. chicken breast	1 dessertspoon light soya sauce
1 teaspoon cornflour	½ teaspoon salt
2 tablespoons cold water	few spring onions, chopped
2 oz. mushrooms	
2 oz. bamboo shoots	
2½ pints hot stock	

1 Shred chicken and mix with cornflour and water.
2 Slice vegetables, cook for 5 minutes in stock.
3 Add chicken and simmer until it turns white.
4 Add soya sauce, salt and spring onions before serving.

Variation

Roast pork and mushroom soup

As above, using 2½ pints stock and adding roast pork, shredded or thinly sliced to each bowl just before serving.

Duck and orange peel soup

cooking time   1–1¼ hours

you will need for 6–8 servings:

1 young duck (4–5 lb.)	2½–3 pints veal (or chicken) stock
little oil	salt
1 oz. dried orange peel	

1 Open duck down centre back and remove inside and backbone.
2 Heat oil in pan and brown duck quickly on all sides. Place in a dish, cut side up.
3 Soak orange peel in cold water for 20 minutes and scrape out pith.
4 Toss peel in a little oil for a couple of minutes.
5 Put peel in duck and moisten with enough stock to fill duck three-quarters full. Add salt to taste.
6 Put dish in pan of water and steam until duck is tender.
7 Take out orange peel and remaining bones of duck. Serve duck in the soup.

Duck and parsnip soup

cooking time   4 hours

you will need for 4 servings:

4 medium-sized parsnips	2 pints water
1 young duckling (2½ lb.)	salt

1 Cut parsnips in half lengthwise.
2 Place duck in a large bowl and cover with the parsnips.
3 Add water, cover with a well-fitting lid, put in a steamer and steam for 4 hours.
4 Season before serving.

Note:

The soup should be very clear and of a subtle flavour.

Chicken chowder

cooking time   2½ hours

you will need for 6 servings:

1 chicken (about 4 lb.)	1 oz. preserved parsnips
5 oz. soft rice	1 tablespoon sesame oil
4 pints water	soya sauce
little oil	salt and pepper
1 oz. rice noodles	spring onions, chopped
½ oz. fresh ginger	little egg for garnish

1 Clean the chicken and, together with the rice, place in a saucepan, cover with water and cook for 2¼ hours.
2 Heat some oil in a saucepan, put in noodles, cook for 2 seconds and remove from heat.
3 Remove chicken, bone it and cut meat into fine slices.
4 Slice ginger and parsnips. Add chicken, ginger and parsnips to the chowder and cook for 3 minutes.
5 Decant the chowder into small individual bowls, sprinkle into each a few drops of sesame oil and soya sauce, a little salt and pepper, and a few drops of the oil in which the noodles were cooked.
6 Stir, garnish each bowl with spring onions, rice noodles and a small dollop of egg.

Variations
Duck chowder
Clean the duck and proceed as described in the recipe for Chicken chowder.
Pork chowder
Proceed as described in the recipe for Chicken chowder, substituting 1 lb. lean pork and 3 lb. pork bones for chicken.
Beef chowder
Proceed as described in the recipe for Chicken chowder, substituting 1 lb. minced beef and 3 lb. beef bones for chicken.

Fish chowder with chrysanthemum petals

cooking time   2½ hours

you will need for 6 servings:

oil for cooking	1 teaspoon cornflour
1½ oz. rice noodles	1 dessertspoon sesame oil
5 oz. soft rice	1 tablespoon soya sauce
2 oz. dried mushrooms	salt and pepper
4½ pints water	1 egg, beaten
1 very large white	a few spring onions,
chrysanthemum	chopped
1 oz. preserved parsnips	2 lettuce hearts,
½ oz. fresh ginger	shredded
1½ lb. filleted sole	

1 Heat the oil in a saucepan, cook the noodles in it for 2 seconds and remove.
2 Place rice and mushrooms in the water, bring to boil and simmer for 2¼ hours.
3 Remove petals from chrysanthemum and rinse them thoroughly under running tap.
4 Slice parsnips and ginger very finely.
5 Cut sole into small pieces.
6 Mix cornflour with water (taken out of the 4¼ pints allowed) and coat the sole with it.
7 Add parsnips, ginger and sole to rice chowder and cook for 2 minutes.
8 Ladle the chowder into small individual bowls, sprinkle into each a few drops of sesame oil and soya sauce, a little salt and pepper and a few drops of the oil in which the rice noodles were cooked.
9 Stir. Garnish each bowl with rice noddles, egg, spring onions and lettuce hearts.
10 Place a few chrysanthemum petals on top. Stir well to blend and serve the chowder piping hot.

Minced chicken and corn chowder with almonds

cooking time   10 minutes

you will need for 4-6 servings:

1 can sweet corn	3 pints hot chicken stock
(cream style)	12 oz. uncooked breast
1 teaspoon cornflour	of chicken, minced
2 tablespoons cold water	2 egg whites, beaten
2 teaspoons salt	2 tablespoons roasted
½ teaspoon pepper	almonds, chopped

1 Mince the corn, to break up the kernels.
2 Blend cornflour with water, add to corn, season with salt and pepper and stir into the stock.
3 Pound the chicken until smooth and add egg whites.
4 Add to corn soup.
5 Bring to the boil again, then simmer very gently for 8-10 minutes. Sprinkle with almonds and serve.

Variation
Minced chicken and corn chowder with ham
As above, using 2 tablespoons of cooked ham, finely shredded, instead of almonds.

Pigeon soup

cooking time   40-45 minutes

you will need for 6 servings:

2 young pigeons, cleaned	salt and pepper
6 dried Chinese mushrooms	½ tablespoon light
1 teaspoon brandy	soya sauce
2½ pints water	

1 Cut pigeons into quarters.
2 Soak mushrooms in hot water and remove stalks.
3 Place all ingredients in double saucepan, bring to boil, season to taste and steam until pigeons are tender. Serve with soya sauce.

Courgette and prawn soup

cooking time   15 minutes

you will need for 4 servings:

1 oz. dried prawns	2 baby marrows
2 pints water	(courgettes)
4 oz. lean pork	1 dessertspoon soya
1 teaspoon salt	sauce

1 Soak the prawns in water, then make up to 2 pints water and bring to boil.
2 Cut pork into thin strips, add to the saucepan, season with salt and simmer for 10 minutes.
3 Peel marrows, cut into small chunks, add to saucepan and cook uncovered for 1½–2 minutes. (Do not allow to simmer any longer as this will cause the courgettes to deteriorate in texture.)
4 Add soya sauce and serve immediately.

Crab soup

cooking time   20 minutes

you will need for 4 servings:

1 large crab	2 cloves garlic, crushed
1½ pints water	4 oz. spring onions,
1 oz. lard (butter or	chopped
olive oil)	2 tomatoes
4 tablespoons sherry	1 dessertspoon cornflour
powdered ginger	1 egg

1 Remove flesh from shell and claws of crab.
2 Put in water, add lard, sherry, pinch of ginger, garlic, spring onions and tomatoes.
3 Thicken with cornflour and simmer for 20 minutes.
4 Beat egg in a soup tureen, bring soup to the boil and pour it over the egg, whisking all the time. Serve at once.

Shark's fin soup

cooking time   6 hours 10 minutes

you will need for 6–8 servings:

12 oz. shark's fins	1 oz. Chinese ham
small piece fresh ginger	1 oz. bamboo shoots
1 clove garlic, crushed	hot chicken stock
cold water	little soya sauce
1 leg of chicken	sesame oil
3 oz. breast of chicken	salt

1 Soak the shark's fins in water for 24 hours.
2 Boil them slowly for 4 hours with ginger and garlic in double the amount of water required to cover them.
3 Drain and remove any flesh on the fins.
4 Put it in a basin, place the chicken leg on top and steam slowly for 2 hours.
5 Remove the chicken leg and any water which may have dropped on the fins.

6 Shred chicken breast, ham and bamboo shoots into fine strips.
7 Put shark's fins into saucepan, pour in enough stock to cover and boil for 5 minutes.
8 Add chicken, ham and bamboo shoots, and simmer for another 5 minutes.
9 Add a few drops of soya sauce, sesame oil and salt to taste and serve.

Scallop and radish soup

cooking time   45 minutes

you will need for 4 servings:

6 oz. plump scallops	2 pints water
large bunch (24) radishes	¾ teaspoon salt

1 Wash and trim scallops and cut into 2–3 round slices.
2 Peel the radishes but do not slice.
3 Put scallops and radishes into a pan with water, bring to the boil, reduce heat and simmer on low heat for 15 minutes.
4 Add salt and simmer for ½ hour.

Pork and broccoli soup, Pekin style

cooking time   17 minutes

you will need for 4 servings

1 lb. broccoli, cut in	1 tablespoon lard
1-inch chunks	½ pint stock (or water
2 pints water	with a bouillon cube)
salt	pepper, freshly ground
8 oz. lean pork, diced	2 tablespoons soya sauce

1 Cook the broccoli in salted water for 5 minutes. *Do not drain.*
2 Fry pork for 2 minutes in lard and add to broccoli and its liquid.
3 Add stock, bring to the boil, simmer for 10 minutes.
4 Season with pepper and soya sauce and serve.

Pork and prawn soup

cooking time   50 minutes

you will need for 4–6 servings:

8 oz. lean pork	½ teaspoon Ve-Tsin
4 oz. giblets	4 oz. prawns, peeled
1 knob green ginger	cooked
salt	8 oz. Chinese cabbage (or
2½ pints water	savoy cabbage) shredded

1 Slice pork and giblets finely and put with ginger and a little salt in water.
2 Simmer for 45 minutes.
3 Add Ve-Tsin and prawns, bring to the boil, add cabbage and boil for 5 minutes.
4 Season to taste and serve.

Shark's fins in whole chicken

cooking time 7 hours

you will need for 6–8 servings:

8 oz. shark's fins	2 oz. Chinese ham
1 small piece fresh ginger	2 oz. bamboo shoots
salt	1 young chicken (about 4 lb.)
1 clove garlic, crushed	3 teaspoons gin
water	veal stock (or chicken stock)
1 chicken leg	

1 Soak shark's fins in water for 24 hours.
2 Boil them slowly for 4 hours, with ginger, salt and garlic in double the amount of water required to cover them.
3 Drain and remove any flesh on the fins.
4 Put it in a basin, place the chicken leg on top and steam slowly for 2 hours.
5 Remove the chicken leg and any water which may have dropped on the fins.
6 Cut Chinese ham and bamboo shoots into fine strips.
7 Clean chicken, open the neck and take out the inside and all the bones, taking care not to break the skin.
8 Pour the gin into the chicken and shake thoroughly.
9 Place shark's fins, bamboo shoots and Chinese ham in the chicken together with enough stock to fill the chicken. Sew up hole at neck.
10 Place chicken in a pan with enough stock to cover. Steam for 1 hour, remove 'stitches' and serve.

Carp and red bean soup

cooking time 2 hours

you will need for 6 servings:

1 carp (1 lb.) (or grey mullet or bass)	½ oz. preserved parsnips, sliced
4 oz. red beans	3½ pints water
1 oz. mushrooms, sliced	salt
1 oz. fresh ginger, sliced	soya sauce

1 Scale and clean the fish.
2 Place beans, mushrooms, carp, ginger and parsnips in water and cook for about 2 hours to reduce the liquid to 2 pints.
3 Add salt to taste and serve with soya sauce.

Sole and sweet cucumber soup

cooking time 5 minutes

you will need for 4 servings:

1 large sole (or plaice), filleted	2 pints water
3 pieces Chinese sweet cucumber	1 dessertspoon soya sauce
4 spring onions	1 dessertspoon peanut oil
	1 white of egg, beaten
	salt and pepper

1 Slice fish into small uniform pieces.
2 Dice the cucumber and chop spring onions.
3 Bring water to boil.
4 Mix fish with soya sauce, oil and sweet cucumber.
5 Pour this mixture into the boiling water. Allow to come to the boil again, remove from heat and whisk in white of egg.
6 Season to taste, sprinkle with spring onions and serve.

Sole and noodle soup

cooking time 1 hour 15 minutes

you will need for 6 servings:

1 sole (1½ lb.)	1½ oz. corn noodles
3 pints water	1 teaspoon cornflour
1½ oz. preserved parsnips	few drops sesame oil
1 oz. dried shrimps	few drops soya sauce
½ oz. fresh ginger	salt and pepper

1 Fillet fish, put the bones in water, add parsnips, shrimps and ginger and cook for 1 hour.
2 Strain and add noodles to the soup. Cook for 12 minutes.
3 Mix cornflour with ¼ pint water and a few drops sesame oil.
4 Cut fish into fine slices, dip in cornflour and water, add to soup and cook for 3 minutes.
5 Add a few more drops sesame oil, soya sauce, salt and pepper to taste and serve.

Fish soup

cooking time 40–45 minutes

you will need for 6–8 servings:

1½ lb. fish (cod, hake)	salt
8 oz. rice	3 tablespoons spring onions, finely chopped
4 pints stock (or water)	1 raw egg (optional) per person
1 tablespoon brandy	
½ tablespoon oil	
1 knob green ginger, finely chopped	

1 Slice fish finely.
2 Wash rice and boil it with half the fish in stock.
3 Simmer for 35–40 minutes until rice softens and makes a thick soup.
4 Combine the rest of the fish with brandy, oil and ginger, season with salt and add to soup.
5 Bring to the boil, sprinkle with spring onions and serve immediately.

Note:

The fish, combined with brandy, oil and ginger, may be placed in individual soup bowls uncooked and the boiling soup poured on it. This is sufficient to cook the fish provided it is sliced finely, and results in excellent flavour. A raw egg can be added to each bowl if liked.

Dried seaweed soup

cooking time   10 minutes

you will need for 4–6 servings:

1 oz. dried seaweed	1 egg, beaten
2½ pints water	few spring onions,
1 teaspoon salt	chopped
4 oz. pork	1 dessertspoon soya sauce

1 Soak the seaweed and wash well.
2 Bring water to the boil and add salt.
3 Cut pork into very thin slices, put in pan and simmer for 5 minutes.
4 Drain seaweed, chop into small pieces, add to stock and simmer for 5 minutes.
5 Add egg and spring onions, after removing the saucepan from heat.
6 Add soya sauce and serve.

Seaweed soup with meat quenelles

cooking time   15 minutes

you will need for 6 servings:

1 lb. lean pork	½ oz. seaweed (Jee Choy)
½ oz. preserved parsnips	2 pints hot stock
2 oz. mushrooms	1 egg, beaten
salt and pepper	little sesame oil

1 Chop pork, parsnips and mushrooms finely.
2 Mix with a little pepper and roll into small balls.
3 Soak seaweed in water for 10 minutes.
4 Strain stock, bring to boil, add seaweed and meat quenelles and cook for 5 minutes.
5 Add egg, sesame oil and salt to taste. Serve at once.

Chinese vermicelli soup with quenelles

cooking time   7–8 minutes

you will need for 4 servings:

1 dessertspoon cornflour	1 oz. Chinese vermicelli
2 tablespoons water	2 pints stock
8 oz. meat, minced (pork for preference)	1 dessertspoon soya sauce
	4 spring onions, chopped

1 Mix the cornflour with water.
2 Blend it into the meat and shape into small balls.
3 Wash vermicelli in warm water, drain and cook in stock for 4 minutes.
4 Add meat quenelles and boil fast for 3 minutes.
5 Add soya sauce and spring onions and serve.

Long and short soup

Long and short soup contains a combination of noodles and meat patties.

cooking time   13–15 minutes

you will need for 4–6 servings:

4 oz. raw pork (or raw prawns), minced	2½ pints chicken (or pork stock)
salt	8 oz. roast pork, or boiled chicken or roast duck, shredded
pastry for patties (see page 17)	
water	1 tablespoon spring onions, finely chopped
noodles (see page 78)	

1 Salt the pork generously and using a coffee spoon, put a small quantity of it on one corner of a small square of pastry prepared as described on page 17.
2 Fold diagonally about half way, using the meat as a seal.
3 Bring the right end of the pastry right across, and after making a half turn seal with a dab of meat on the first fold.
4 Do likewise with the left end. (It is important that the three ends of the pastry should be left free and loose).
5 Drop these patties into a pan of boiling water and boil for 5 minutes.
6 Do likewise with the noodles prepared as described on page 78 and boil for 8 minutes, making sure the noodles do not stick together.
7 Drain, place in a serving bowl, add boiling stock, roast pork or chicken or duck.
8 Sprinkle with spring onions and serve.

Chinese Wun Tun soup

cooking time   7 minutes

you will need for 6 servings:

Wun Tun (see page 17)	1 dessertspoon soya sauce
1½ lb. pork	1 dessertspoon brandy
salt	1 teaspoon oil
1 oz. dried mushrooms	1 egg
6 oz. prawns, shelled	1 egg, beaten
½ teaspoon Ve-Tsin	water
4 oz. spring onions, chopped	2½ pints hot pork stock (or chicken stock)
1 dessertspoon cornflour	

Make the *Wun Tun* in advance.

1 Mince the pork and season with salt to taste.
2 Scald and shred the mushrooms.
3 Cut the pastry into 3-inch squares (see page 17).
4 Combine pork, mushrooms, prawns, Ve-Tsin and three-quarters of the spring onions, cornflour, soya, brandy, oil and 1 egg. Blend well.
5 Place a quantity of this mixture on the pastry.
6 Fold over, seal with egg and round off the edge of the Wun Tun.
7 Boil fast for 7 minutes in plenty of water, keeping the pan uncovered.

8 Drain and serve in bowls of hot, strained stock, allowing 4–5 Wun Tun per bowl. Sprinkle with the remaining spring onions.

Pastry for noodles and patties (Wun Tun)

cooking time   as individual recipe

you will need for 4–6 servings:

1 lb. plain flour   water
2 eggs

1 Mix flour and eggs together and add enough water to make pliable dough.
2 Roll out paper thin.
3 For the patties, cut pastry into pieces 2-inches square. For the noodles, fold over 6–8 times, dusting the layers with plain flour, and cut into strips ⅛-inch wide.

Note:

Both noodles and ready made patties, called Wun Tun, are obtainable in shops.

Liver soup

cooking time   5 minutes

you will need for 4 servings:

3 oz. liver   2 pints stock (or water)
1 teaspoon cornflour   1 teaspoon sesame oil
2 tablespoons cold water 1 dessertspoon soya
4 oz. spinach (or small   sauce
   packet of frozen spinach)

1 Cut the liver into slices.
2 Mix cornflour with water and coat the liver.
3 Wash spinach, unless frozen spinach is used.
4 Bring stock to boil with sesame oil and soya sauce.
5 Add spinach, cook for 2 minutes.
6 Add liver, cook for another 3 minutes and serve.

Beef and turnip soup

cooking time   35 minutes

you will need for 4 servings:

8 oz. beef   2 pieces dried tangerine
1½–2 pints water   peel
1 teaspoon salt   2 slices green ginger
2 small turnips   1 dessertspoon soya
               sauce

1 Cut the meat into slices.
2 Bring water to the boil and add meat.
3 Season with salt and simmer for 5 minutes.
4 Peel and dice turnips and add to the water together with tangerine peel, ginger and soya sauce.
5 Simmer for 30 minutes and serve.

Giblet soup

cooking time   13 minutes

you will need for 4–6 servings:

8 oz. giblets   2½ pints water
4 oz. lean pork   1 teaspoon salt
½ Chinese cabbage (or 1 dessertspoon light
  Savoy cabbage)   soya sauce

1 Slice giblets and pork into thin pieces and shred cabbage.
2 Bring water to the boil, add pork, giblets and salt.
3 Simmer gently for 10 minutes, add cabbage.
4 Cook for 3 minutes, add soya sauce and serve.

Variation

Giblet and Chinese mushroom soup

As above, adding at the same time as pork and giblets 8–12 small dried Chinese mushrooms, having previously soaked them in hot water until soft, and drained them.

Beef and tomato soup

cooking time   10 minutes

you will need for 4 servings:

1½ lb. tomatoes   1 teaspoon salt
1 dessertspoon sugar 1½ pints water
8 oz. beef (rump)   1 dessertspoon soya
2 teaspoons peanut (or   sauce
  olive oil)   1 dessertspoon cornflour
2 cloves garlic, crushed 2 tablespoons cold water

1 Skin tomatoes and cut into quarters, sprinkle with sugar and leave to stand.
2 Cut meat into thin strips.
3 Heat oil in saucepan, add garlic and salt.
4 When the garlic is browned, add water and bring to boil.
5 Add tomatoes and steak, cook for 5 minutes, add soya sauce.
6 Mix cornflour with water, stir into the soup, simmer, stirring to thicken, and serve.

Steak and beetroot soup

cooking time   25 minutes

you will need for 6 servings:

8 oz. steak   2 pieces tangerine peel
2½ pints water   2 large beetroots
salt   1 dessertspoon light
2 slices green ginger   soya sauce

1 Cut the steak into small strips.
2 Bring water to the boil, add salt to taste, ginger, tangerine peel and steak.
3 Simmer gently for 15 minutes.
4 Cut beetroot into small slices, add to the stock and cook for 10 minutes.
5 Add soya sauce and serve.

Kidney and cucumber soup

cooking time   3 minutes

you will need for 4 servings:

3 lamb's kidneys	1½ pints stock (or hot
1 heaped teaspoon	water)
cornflour	½ large cucumber, sliced
3 tablespoons water	1 dessertspoon light
2 oz. fresh mushrooms	soya sauce
1 dessertspoon lard	
(or oil)	

1 Trim kidneys, remove all gristle, cut into thin slices.
2 Mix with cornflour and water.
3 Slice mushrooms and fry quickly with kidneys in lard or oil, for 2 minutes.
4 Add stock, bring to boil, and add cucumber.
5 Simmer for 1 minute, add soya sauce, and serve.

Brain soup

cooking time   10 minutes

you will need for 4 servings:

3 pairs pig's (or calf's, or	1 oz. mushrooms, sliced
lamb's) brains	2 tablespoons sherry
warm, salted water	few spring onions,
1 oz. turnips, grated	chopped
2 pints white stock	salt and pepper

1 Wash brains thoroughly in salted warm water.
2 Boil turnips in stock for 5 minutes.
3 Add mushrooms and brains and rest of ingredients.
4 Bring to the boil, simmer for 5 minutes and serve.

Meat cake soup

cooking time   45 minutes

you will need for 4 servings:

4 oz. raw pork, finely	2 oz. water chestnuts,
chopped	chopped
½ teaspoon salt	1 egg, raw
½ teaspoon pepper	1–1½ pints light stock
1½ teaspoons soya sauce	(or water)

1 Season pork with salt, pepper and soya sauce.
2 Add water chestnuts, mix well.
3 Add egg to bind, stir and shape the mixture into a thick flat cake.
4 Pack the pork cake into a double boiler, add stock or water, cover tightly and cook over boiling water for 45 minutes.

Note:

Finely minced beef may be used instead of pork, and the meat may be fashioned into small cakes instead of one large one.

Minced pork soup

cooking time   45 minutes

you will need for 4–6 servings:

8 oz. rice	1 tablespoon light soya
6 pints water	sauce
1 knob dried salt cabbage	1 tablespoon brandy
(Hahm Choy)	1 teaspoon oil
1 lb. pork	1 tablespoon spring
salt	onions, finely chopped

1 Wash rice and boil in water.
2 Simmer until rice softens, absorbs the water and makes a thick soup (about 40 minutes).
3 Blanch the salt cabbage.
4 Mince pork and cabbage together and season with salt.
5 Blend in soya sauce, brandy and oil, and mix well.
6 Roll the meat into small balls and add to soup.
7 Bring to boil, poach for a few minutes, sprinkle with spring onions and serve.

Pork and mushroom soup

cooking time   7–8 minutes

you will need for 4 servings:

2 oz. lean pork	1¼ pints stock (or water)
1 teaspoon cornflour	3 spring onions
2 tablespoons cold water	1 dessertspoon light
2 oz. fresh mushrooms	soya sauce
(or dried mushrooms),	1 teaspoon lard
sliced	

1 Slice meat finely and mix with cornflour and water.
2 Bring mushrooms to boil in stock.
3 Add meat and other ingredients and stir gently.
4 Simmer for 5 minutes and serve.

Note:

When dried mushrooms are used, they should be soaked in warm water before cooking.

Scallop and pork soup

cooking time   6–7 minutes

you will need for 6 servings:

6 oz. lean pork, cut in	1 teaspoon Chinese wine
thin slices	(or sherry)
2 teaspoons cornflour	1 teaspoon salt
1 tablespoon soya	3–4 scallops
sauce	3 pints water

1 Sprinkle pork with cornflour, soya sauce, wine and half the salt.
2 Wash scallops in running water, trim off tough edges and cut each scallop into 3–4 round slices.

3 Put scallops in a pan with water. Bring to the boil, reduce heat and simmer for 3–4 minutes.
4 Add pork, bring to the boil. Taste for seasoning; if necessary, add the rest of salt. Cook for 2 minutes and serve.

Pork and cuttlefish soup

cooking time   3 hours

you will need for 4–6 servings:

3 oz. dried cuttlefish (or canned awabi)	3 pints stock (or water) salt and pepper
1 lb. pork	few spring onions, chopped
4 oz. fresh mushrooms	

1 Soak cuttlefish in warm water for 3 hours and cut into strips.
2 Cut pork into small squares.
3 Slice mushrooms.
4 Put fish, mushrooms and meat into stock, bring to boil.
5 Cover and simmer gently for 3 hours.
6 Season with salt and pepper, sprinkle with spring onions and serve.

Pig's trotter soup

cooking time   3 hours 45 minutes

you will need for 6 servings:

4 oz. black soya beans	1 dessertspoon light soya sauce
3 pints water	2 slices green ginger
2 pieces dried tangerine peel	1 teaspoon salt
2 trotters, singed and cleaned	

1 Soak beans in water for 4–5 hours.
2 Bring them to the boil in water with tangerine peel, simmer for 45 minutes.
3 Add trotters, soya sauce, ginger and salt, simmer 3 hours until trotters are cooked.
4 Drain the trotters, slice into small pieces and serve with soup.

Note:

This preparation can also be served as an aspic.

Pork and lotus root soup

cooking time   2 hours

you will need for 6–8 servings:

1 lb. lean pork	4 pints water
2 oz. dried lotus roots	salt
1 oz. mushrooms	soya sauce

1 Place all ingredients in saucepan (except soya sauce).
2 Cook for about 2 hours, this should reduce the liquid to 2½ pints.
3 Remove pork, cut into strips 1-inch long and ¼-inch thick.
4 Put strips back into soup, add salt and serve with soya sauce.

Lotus seed soup

cooking time   32 minutes

you will need for 6 servings:

3 oz. preserved persimmons	1 oz. preserved sweet lotus seeds
1 oz. Jerusalem artichokes, sliced	2 oz. preserved sweet melon
2 pints hot water	cane sugar

1 Wash and soak persimmons and artichokes in warm water for 30 minutes.
2 Bring water to boil, put in lotus seeds and artichokes.
3 Simmer for 30 minutes.
4 Slice melon and persimmons, add to the saucepan and cook for 2 minutes.
5 Add cane sugar to taste and serve in small bowls.

Fresh lotus seed and duck soup

cooking time   2 hours

you will need for 6–8 servings:

1 duck (about 2½ lb.)	1 dessertspoon sherry
3½ pints water	1 can fresh lotus seeds
2 oz. bamboo shoots	1 teaspoon sesame oil
2 oz. fresh mushrooms	1 teaspoon soya sauce
1 oz. water chestnuts	salt and pepper
1 teaspoon cornflour	

1 Bone duck and boil the bones in water for 2 hours. Slice duck meat finely.
2 Shred bamboo shoots, mushrooms and water chestnuts and mix together.
3 Dilute cornflour with ¼ pint water, add sherry and pour over duck.
4 Remove bones from soup, then add water chestnuts, bamboo shoots, mushrooms, lotus seed and duck meat.
5 Cook for 3 minutes, add sesame oil and soya sauce.
6 Season with salt and pepper and serve.

Water lily soup

cooking time   30 minutes

you will need for 4–6 servings:

6 dried oysters	1 teaspoon salt
8 pieces dried water lily roots (or 6 oz. canned)	1 dessertspoon soya sauce
4 oz. pork	few spring onions, chopped
3 pints water	

1 Soak oysters in warm water and clean.
2 Soak lily roots (unnecessary if canned lily roots are used) and cut into halves.
3 Cut pork into very thin slices.
4 Place all ingredients, except spring onions to boil and simmer until lily roots are tender.
5 Garnish with spring onions and serve.

Soup with stuffed cucumbers

cooking time   30–35 minutes

you will need for 4 servings:

1–2 cucumbers	1 tablespoon cornflour
4–6 oz. raw pork, minced	4 oz. mushrooms, with
1 egg, beaten	small flat caps
salt	2 pints light stock (or
1 tablespoon Chinese	water with a bouillon
wine (or sherry)	cube)
	pinch Ve-Tsin

1 Peel cucumbers, cut into 1½-inch chunks and with a small ball scoop carefully hollow out, to make little 'cups', i.e. without digging right through.
2 Put pork in a bowl, add egg, pinch salt, wine and cornflour. Blend well and use the mixture for stuffing the cucumber 'cups'. Pack the stuffed cucumbers, standing upright, into a pan, cover each with a mushroom cap.
3 Carefully add ½ pint lightly salted stock, cover the pan and simmer for ½ hour.
4 Bring remainder of stock to the boil, add Ve-Tsin. Pour into the pan containing cucumbers, cook for 1 minute and serve.

Chinese consommé

cooking time   20 minutes

you will need for 6 servings:

1 boiling fowl	1 tablespoon soya sauce
1 dessertspoon salt	little ham, chopped
6 oz. pork	spring onions, chopped
4 pints water	

1 Clean chicken and rub with salt.
2 Cut pork into 3 or 4 pieces.
3 Bring water to the boil, add pork and simmer for 10 minutes.
4 Add salt, soya sauce and chicken.
5 Boil fast for 10 minutes, remove from heat and leave the chicken to stand until cold.
6 Remove the breast and shred finely.
7 Add it to the strained soup together with the chopped ham and spring onions and serve, hot or cold.

Meat and Poultry

Pork is the meat which figures mainly on Chinese menus. Poultry takes the next place. Beef is used in some areas and there are many recipes for preparing it. Mutton seldom makes an appearance on a Chinese table.

Chinese recipes offer a wonderful opportunity for preserving economy and yet producing delicious dishes. Most recipes call for relatively small amounts of meat and, as meat is normally cooked with vegetables, a little goes a long way. It is not uncommon for a Chinese housewife to bring home from the market a few ounces of meat or chicken and invent a dish in which the combined flavours of several ingredients are blended to provide an interesting and satisfying meal at small cost.

Stewed pork with lily petals

cooking time   1 hour 20 minutes

you will need for 6 servings:

1½ lb. pork	1 teaspoon salt
2 cloves garlic	1 teaspoon sugar
oil	strained stock to cover
1 teaspoon thick sweet	4 oz. lily petals
sauce (Tak Chu Yow)	

1 Cut pork into strips 2-inches by ½-inch.
2 Pound the garlic, toss in a hot oiled pan for 1 minute and remove.
3 Place pork in the pan, add thick sweet sauce, salt, sugar and stock.
4 Simmer gently for 1 hour with the lid on.
5 Add lily petals. Simmer for a further 20 minutes and serve.

Fried minced pork

cooking time   10–12 minutes

you will need for 4 servings:

5 oz. pork, minced	stock to cover
2 oz. water chestnuts	1 teaspoon cornflour
2 oz. mushrooms	2 tablespoons water
2 oz. bamboo shoots	1 teaspoon sesame oil
salt and pepper	soya sauce
sugar	

1 Combine pork, water chestnuts, mushrooms and bamboo shoots.
2 Add a little salt and chop all together into fine pieces.
3 Place in hot oiled pan and cook for 5 minutes.
4 Add salt and pepper, and sugar to taste, as well as stock.
5 Simmer for 5 minutes.
6 Add cornflour mixed with water, sesame oil, and soya sauce to taste. Season, cook for 1 minute and serve.

Steamed minced pork

cooking time   10 minutes

you will need for 4 servings:

10 oz. pork	1 oz. preserved parsnips
4 oz. water chestnuts	½ oz. lichen (Wun Yee)
1 oz. mushrooms	salt and pepper
1½ oz. preserved	½ teaspoon sugar
cucumbers	few drops sesame oil

1 Combine pork, water chestnuts, mushrooms, cucumbers, parsnips and lichen, and chop them together.
2 Add salt, pepper, sugar and sesame oil, blend well.
3 Place in a dish. Steam for 10 minutes and serve.

Bean curd with minced pork

cooking time   13–14 minutes

you will need for 4 servings:

½ lb. pork, minced	small pinch chilli paste
1 teaspoon flour	(optional)
1 tablespoon Chinese wine	1 teaspoon dark soya
(or sherry)	sauce
salt and pepper	pinch sugar
Ve-Tsin	pinch Chinese anise-
2 tablespoons peanut oil	pepper
2 spring onions, finely	1 teaspoon cornflour
chopped	2–3 tablespoons stock
2 cakes fresh bean curd,	(or water)
diced	

1 Sprinkle pork with flour, wine, salt and pepper to taste and a pinch Ve-Tsin.
2 Fry in oil with spring onions for 2–3 minutes.
3 Add bean curd and the rest of ingredients except cornflour. Cover and simmer for 10 minutes.
4 Dilute cornflour in stock, stir into the pan, cook for 1 minute and serve.

Fried meat balls

cooking time   10 minutes

you will need for 4 servings:

5 oz. water chestnuts	flour
9 oz. pork, minced	2 eggs, beaten
salt and pepper	oil for cooking
sesame oil	

1 Crush water chestnuts with blade of knife.
2 Mix with pork.
3 Season with salt and pepper.
4 Add a few drops of sesame oil and chop together.
5 Shape into balls about the size of a walnut.
6 Roll the balls in flour until well covered, then dip in egg.
7 Place in saucepan of boiling oil and cook for 10 minutes.

Tung-Po pork

cooking time   1 hour 45 minutes

you will need for 4 servings:

1 lb. pork	1 teaspoon sugar
1 pint water	2 lb. spinach (or cabbage)
2 tablespoons soya sauce	shredded
1 dessertspoon sherry	salt

1 Boil pork in water for 15 minutes, then strain water into a bowl, leaving pork in the pan.
2 Add to pork soya sauce, sherry and sugar. Simmer gently, turning all the time to ensure even browning. (If the pan juices tend to dry up, add a few teaspoons of the water in which the pork was boiled.)
3 Simmer gently for 20 minutes and leave to stand until cold.
4 Cut the pork into uniform oblong pieces, arrange them neatly in an oven-proof dish.
5 Steam for 1 hour, either in a steamer or a pan of hot water.
6 Scramble the spinach in fat taken from the pork (allowing the same time as for scrambling an egg).
7 Season with salt. Heap the vegetables on the pork, put out on to a deep dish and serve, with the pan juices from the pork poured over.

Minced pork with sweet corn

cooking time   6–7 minutes

you will need for 4 servings:

4 oz. raw pork, minced	1 can cream-style sweet
½ teaspoon Ve-Tsin	corn
1 teaspoon light coloured	water
soya sauce	2 egg whites
salt	1 tablespoon cooked ham,
1 teaspoon cornflour	minced

1 Sprinkle pork with Ve-Tsin, soya sauce, a pinch of salt and cornflour and mix well.
2 Pour contents of sweet corn can into a saucepan, add equal amount of water and heat. As soon as boiling is established, add pork and cook together for 5 minutes, stirring constantly.
3 Beat egg whites with a tablespoon cold water, gradually add to the saucepan, stirring all the time.
4 As soon as the egg whites are blended in and set, transfer to a heated serving dish.
5 Sprinkle the top with ham and serve.

Variation

Minced chicken with sweet corn
As recipe above, substituting chicken for pork.

21

Green peas with minced pork

cooking time   10–12 minutes

you will need for 4–6 servings:

½ lb. pork, minced
2 tablespoons flour
1 teaspoon Chinese wine (or sherry)
1 teaspoon light soya sauce
Ve-Tsin
salt and pepper
large packet frozen peas

1 cup water, boiling
2 tablespoons peanut oil
3 spring onions cut 1–1½-inch lengths
1–2 slices ginger
½ teaspoon cornflour
1–2 tablespoons water, cold

1 Sprinkle pork with flour, wine, soya sauce, small pinch Ve-Tsin, and salt and pepper to taste. Mix well.
2 Cook peas in salted boiling water for 2 minutes and drain.
3 Heat oil, fry onion and ginger for 2–3 minutes, until they render up their flavours and discard them.
4 Fry pork in this onion and ginger flavoured oil for 5 minutes, stirring constantly. Add peas, cook for 1 minute.
5 Dilute cornflour in cold water, stir into the pan, cook for 1 minute and serve.

Pork with spinach

cooking time   5 minutes

you will need for 4 servings:

8 oz. cold roast pork
oil for cooking (or pork dripping)
3 lb. spinach (or 1 large packet frozen spinach)
salt

stock to cover
1 teaspoon cornflour
2 tablespoons cold water
sesame oil
1 teaspoon soya sauce

1 Cut the pork into neat slices.
2 Toss quickly in a hot pan in a little oil. (do not cook for more than 1 minute.)
3 Add spinach, salt to taste and stock.
4 Simmer for 2 minutes.
5 Add cornflour diluted with water, sesame oil, soya sauce and a little pork dripping.
6 Cook for 2 minutes and serve.

Pork with bean sprouts

cooking time   4 minutes

you will need for 4 servings:

oil for cooking
8 oz. pork, finely sliced
1½ lb. bean sprouts
hot stock to cover
salt and pepper
soya sauce
½ teaspoon cornflour

2 tablespoons cold water
½ teaspoon sesame oil
2 small pieces Chinese preserved cucumber, sliced
2–3 spring onions, chopped

1 Heat oil in a pan and sauté the pork for 1 minute.
2 Add bean sprouts and stock.

3 Simmer with lid on for 1 minute.
4 Season with salt, pepper and soya sauce.
5 Cook for 1 minute.
6 Add cornflour diluted with water, sesame oil, cucumbers and spring onions.
7 Cook for a further minute and serve.

Fried pork

cooking time   7–8 minutes

you will need for 4 servings:

8 oz. lean pork
1 teaspoon cornflour
2 tablespoons cold water
4 oz. bamboo shoots

4 oz. beans (or cabbage, or other available fresh vegetable)
½ oz. lard (or oil)
1 tablespoon soya sauce
spring onions, chopped

1 Cut the meat into thin strips and coat with cornflour diluted with water.
2 Fry bamboo shoots and beans in lard for 5 minutes.
3 Add pork and fry together for 2–3 minutes.
4 Add a little water if the mixture sticks to the pan.
5 Season with soya sauce. Sprinkle with spring onions and serve.

Crisp twice-cooked pork

cooking time   45 minutes

you will need for 4 servings:

12 oz. belly of pork
1 tablespoon soya sauce
1 tablespoon Chinese wine (or sherry)
½ teaspoon star aniseed

1 teaspoon sugar
oil for deep frying
1 egg, beaten
4 oz. cornflour

1 Put pork into a pan, sprinkle with soya sauce, wine, aniseed and sugar. Bring to the boil. Cover with a well fitting lid and simmer gently for 40 minutes.
2 Heat oil. Cut pork into bite-size pieces, dip in egg and cornflour, shake off any surplus of cornflour.
3 Deep fry pieces of pork for a few minutes, until crisp and golden. Drain and serve at once.

Note:

The pan juices left from braising the pork can be reheated and served separately.

Braised pork

cooking time   1 hour 15 minutes

you will need for 4 servings:

1 lb. pork
½ pint cold water
1 tablespoon soya sauce
1 dessertspoon sherry

1 teaspoon sugar
pinch salt
8 oz. mushrooms, sliced

1 Cut pork into uniform square pieces.
2 Put in water, bring to boil, skim and simmer for 30 minutes.
3 Strain off the stock into a bowl leaving the pork in a pan.
4 Add to pork, soya sauce and cook gently for 10 minutes, turning constantly to brown on all sides.
5 Add sherry, sugar and salt. Stir and add stock.
6 Cook for 20 minutes, stirring from time to time.
7 Add mushrooms, slipping them under the pork and simmer gently for 10 minutes. This dish can be served hot or cold.

Pork with celery and bean sprouts

cooking time   45 minutes

you will need for 4–6 servings:

4 oz. fresh bean sprouts	1 lb. celery, cut in
3 tablespoons oil	chunks 1-inch long
2 teaspoons salt	1 large onion, coarsely cut
½ teaspoon pepper	1 tablespoon treacle
1 lb. pork (shoulder), diced	1 pint boiling stock
	3 tablespoons cornflour
2–3 tablespoons soya sauce	2 tablespoons cold water

1 Pick over and wash the bean sprouts, then leave to drain.
2 Heat oil, salt and pepper together.
3 Add pork and brown very quickly, to seal in juices.
4 Cook, stirring all the time, for 7–8 minutes.
5 Add soya sauce, stir, add celery and onions and cook together for 3 minutes.
6 Mix treacle with stock, add to pan, stir, cover and simmer gently for 30 minutes.
7 Add bean sprouts, mix, cook for 3 minutes.
8 Blend cornflour with water, add to pan, cook, stirring until sauce thickens and serve.

Sweet and sour pork

cooking time   15 minutes

you will need for 4 servings:

1 lb. pork (lean and fat)	2 oz. cornflour
salt	lard (or oil) for deep
1 egg, beaten	frying

1 Skin the pork and cut into 1-inch cubes, season with salt.
2 Dip cubes in egg, then cornflour and deep fry in lard. (The pork is cooked when it rises to the surface and acquires a lovely golden colour.)
3 Heap on a dish and serve covered with sweet and sour sauce prepared in the following manner:

Sweet sour sauce

you will need for 4 servings:

2 slices pineapple (or 4 oz. Chinese mixed pickles), diced	½ tablespoon tomato sauce
oil	1 dessertspoon cornflour
pinch ground ginger	1½ teaspoons soya sauce
2 tablespoons vinegar	1 teaspoon brandy
1½ tablespoons sugar	½ pint water
	2 oz. spring onions, finely chopped

1 Fry pineapple in very little oil sprinkled with ginger.
2 Mix vinegar, sugar, tomato sauce, cornflour, soya sauce and brandy together.
3 Stir, blend in water and add mixture to the fried pineapple.
4 Simmer gently for 5 minutes, stirring all the time. (If the sauce becomes too thick, add a little more water.)
5 At the last moment, add spring onions and pour this sauce over the pork.

Fried pork and cucumber

cooking time   10 minutes

you will need for 4 servings:

1 teaspoon cornflour	½ cucumber
2 tablespoons cold water	1 oz. oil
8 oz. lean pork	1 tablespoon soya sauce

1 Mix cornflour with water.
2 Cut meat into thin uniform slices and mix with cornflour paste.
3 Cut cucumber in slices and fry in oil for 3 minutes.
4 Add meat and fry together for 5 minutes.
5 Add soya sauce, simmer for 2–3 minutes and serve.

Variations
Fried pork and asparagus
As above, substituting equivalent amount (½ bunch or small can) of asparagus for cucumber.
Fried pork and seakale
Substitute equivalent amount of seakale for cucumber and proceed as above.
Fried pork and French beans
Substitute equivalent amount of French beans for cucumber and proceed as above.

Fried spiced pork

cooking time   5 minutes

you will need for 4 servings:

8 oz. pork	½ oz. Chinese spice (Ng Heung Fun)
flour	2 tablespoons oil
salt and pepper	
sherry	

1 Cut pork into thin slices and roll in flour.
2 Season with salt and pepper and sprinkle with a little sherry and Chinese spice.
3 Mix together, then dredge with flour.
4 Leave to macerate for 20–30 minutes. Heat oil in pan and fry the pork for 5 minutes.

Pork and peanuts

cooking time   12 minutes

you will need for 4–6 servings:

5 oz. peanuts, shelled	1 teaspoon cornflour
salt	1 clove garlic, crushed
2 dessertspoons oil	1 dessertspoon oyster
1½ lb. pork	sauce
5 oz. fresh mushrooms	¼ pint water
2 oz. celery	spring onions, finely
1 dessertspoon soya sauce	chopped
1 dessertspoon brandy	

1 Blanch peanuts, sprinkle with salt and fry briskly in very little oil, taking care not to burn them.
2 As soon as they turn golden, remove and drain on greaseproof paper.
3 Cut pork into small dice.
4 Chop mushrooms and celery.
5 Combine pork, soya, brandy, cornflour and salt. Mix well.
6 Heat oil in a pan with garlic, add pork and cook briskly, stirring all the time.
7 Add oyster sauce, mushrooms and celery. Simmer for 5 minutes, stirring all the time.
8 Add peanuts and stir well.
9 Add water to dilute the gravy, bring to the boil, sprinkle with spring onions and serve.

Steamed pork with bean curd

cooking time   45 minutes

you will need for 4 servings:

1 lb. shoulder of pork,	1½ teaspoons cornflour
thinly cut	3 tablespoons cold water
2 cubes bean curd	1 teaspoon soya sauce
½ teaspoon Ve-Tsin	

1 Put the pork on a steaming dish (shallow casserole or even a soup plate will do).
2 Mix all the other ingredients and blend into the pork.
3 Place in a pan, standing the dish on a grid.
4 Fill the pan with boiling water, without allowing it to touch the grid.
5 Cover, bring to the boil, steam for 45 minutes and serve.

Pork and cauliflower

cooking time   12 minutes

you will need for 4 servings:

12 oz. pork	salt
1 smallish cauliflower	1 dessertspoon oil
1 dessertspoon soya sauce	1 knob green ginger,
1 dessertspoon brandy	sliced
	½ pint water

1 Cut meat into thin slices and divide cauliflower into little flowerets.
2 Add soya, brandy and a pinch of salt to the meat.
3 Heat oil in a pan with ginger, then add meat and stir well. Cook for 5 minutes.
4 Add cauliflower, stirring all the time.
5 Add water, simmer for 5 minutes and serve.

Variations:
Pork and cabbage
Substitute equivalent amount of cabbage for cauliflower and proceed as described in the above recipe.
Pork and peas
Substitute 1 lb. peas for cauliflower and add 1¼ pints of water instead of ¼ pint. Simmer together for 10 minutes. The gravy can be thickened with a little cornflour, if required.

Pork with fresh mushrooms

cooking time   12–13 minutes

you will need for 4 servings:

1 lb. shoulder of pork	8 oz. fresh mushrooms,
2 tablespoons oil	sliced
2 tablespoons soya sauce	½ teaspoon salt
¼ pint boiling water	1 tablespoon cornflour
	3 tablespoons cold water

1 Cut the pork into very thin slices 1½-inch square.
2 Heat the oil and brown the pork briskly.
3 Add soya sauce and boiling water, stir well.
4 Cover the pan and cook for 5 minutes.
5 Add mushrooms, stir, cook for 3 minutes. Season with salt.
6 Blend cornflour with water and stir into the pan.
7 Simmer, stirring constantly, until the sauce thickens (2–3 minutes, usually) and serve.

Pork with red bean curd

cooking time   3½ hours

you will need for 4–6 servings:

1½ lb. pork (flank)	1 tablespoon oil
1 teaspoon salt	2 tablespoons red bean
1 tablespoon soya sauce	curd
2 medium-sized potatoes	4 pieces Chinese aniseed
2 eggs	1 lettuce
4 tablespoons milk	

1 Bone the meat, sprinkle with salt and brush with soya sauce.
2 Peel and slice the potatoes.
3 Whisk eggs with milk and fry several very thin pancake omelettes.
4 Cut these into pieces of uniform size.
5 Heat oil in pan, fry the meat briskly for 10 minutes until it browns nicely.
6 Allow to cool and cut into uniform slices ½-inch thick.
7 Add red bean curd and mix well.

8 Grease a bowl or deep dish lightly, put in a layer of meat, then a layer of potato slices, following with a layer of egg pancake. Repeat these layers until the dish is full.

9 Scatter aniseed on top.

10 Place the dish in a pan of hot water and steam for 3 hours.

11 Serve in a dish lined with crisp lettuce leaves.

Steamed pork with ground rice

cooking time   2 hours

you will need for 4 servings:

1 lb. pork, fairly fat	2 tablespoons cooking
3 tablespoons soya sauce	sherry
	8 oz. ground rice

1 Cut pork into neat pieces, sprinkle with soya sauce, and sherry and leave to macerate for 20–30 minutes.

2 Bake the rice slightly, to dry off, and roll the pork in it.

3 Place in a basin, cover with a lid, stand in a pan of water and steam for 1½ hours, adding water to pan if necessary.

Roast pork with apple crescents

cooking time   30 minutes

you will need for 4 servings:

1 lb. lean pork	pinch Ve-Tsin
2 tablespoons sugar	few drops cochineal
1 dessertspoon light soya	colouring
sauce	1 tablespoon sesame oil
1 tablespoon red soya	1 tablespoon honey
bean paste	2–3 apples
pinch salt	lemon juice

1 Cut the pork with the grain into long strips.

2 Put sugar, soya sauce, bean paste (bean curd), salt, Ve-Tsin and cochineal into a bowl.

3 Mix well, put in pork strips and leave to steep in the flavouring for 1 hour.

4 Skewer the meat and either grill on a high flame or suspend from the shelf bars in the hottest possible oven (500°F.–Gas 9) and roast for 15 minutes. (Whatever method you choose, catch all the juices in a drip pan, to be used as gravy.)

5 Mix sesame oil with honey, brush the meat with the mixture and continue to cook for 10 minutes.

6 Meanwhile, peel and core the apples, cut into round slices, then cut each slice in half and trim into a 'crescent'.

7 Brush with lemon juice to prevent discoloration.

8 Slice the meat thinly across the grain, arrange on a heated ovenproof serving dish overlapping with apple half moons, pour the gravy from the drip pan over the dish.

9 Return to the oven for 5 minutes and serve.

Pork with bean sprouts and oyster sauce

cooking time   10 minutes

you will need for 4 servings:

12 oz. lean pork	½ oz. fresh ginger,
1 teaspoon soya sauce	finely chopped
pinch sugar	½ oz. spring onions,
2 teaspoons cornflour	finely chopped
pinch salt	1 tablespoon peanut oil
4 oz. bean sprouts	1 tablespoon oyster sauce
	2 tablespoons water

1 Cut the pork first into thin slices then into strips. Sprinkle with soya sauce, sugar, 1 teaspoon cornflour and salt. Mix well.

2 If canned bean sprouts are used, drain thoroughly.

3 Fry ginger and onions lightly in oil for 1 minute. Add pork and fry for 5 minutes, stirring constantly.

4 Add bean sprouts and cook together for 2 minutes.

5 Blend in oyster sauce.

6 Dilute remaining cornflour with water, stir into the pan, simmer for 12 minutes to thicken the sauce and serve.

Pork and courgettes

cooking time   10–12 minutes

you will need for 4 servings:

12 oz. pork	1 dessertspoon oil
1 clove garlic	3–4 small courgettes,
1 dessertspoon soya sauce	finely sliced
1 dessertspoon brandy	1 teaspoon oyster sauce
1 dessertspoon cornflour	½ pint water
salt	

1 Cut the meat into very thin slices.

2 Chop garlic, sprinkle on the meat, add soya, brandy, cornflour and a pinch of salt.

3 Mix thoroughly.

4 Heat oil in pan, add meat and cook briskly for 5 minutes, stirring constantly to avoid burning.

5 Add courgettes and oyster sauce, cook for 5 minutes.

6 Add water, bring to the boil and serve.

Pork omelette

cooking time   7 minutes

you will need for 4 servings:

1 tablespoon oil	6 eggs
1 small onion, chopped	salt and pepper
6 oz. lean pork, minced	

1 Heat a greased pan and cook the onions for ½ minute.

2 Add pork and cook for 5 minutes.

3 Beat eggs, season with salt and pepper.

4 Add to the pan and cook for 1½ minutes shaking the pan from time to time. Serve at once.

Steamed pork with preserved vegetables

cooking time   15 minutes

you will need for 4 servings:

10 oz. lean pork	1 teaspoon cornflour
salt and pepper	2 tablespoons cold water
1 dessertspoon sugar	2 oz. Chinese preserved
1 dessertspoon gin	vegetables (Tong Choy)
few drops sesame oil	

1 Cut the pork into very fine slices.
2 Season with salt and pepper, sprinkle with sugar, gin and sesame oil and bind with cornflour mixed with water.
3 Blend thoroughly, place preserved vegetables on top and steam for 15 minutes, standing the dish in a pan of hot water.

Note:

Fresh vegetables can be used instead of preserved.

Pork cubes with sweet sour sauce

cooking time   7–8 minutes

you will need for 4 servings:

1 lb. lean pork	sweet sour sauce
salt and pepper	(see page 23)
flour	4 oz. Chinese pickled
2 eggs, beaten	onions
oil for deep frying	few drops sesame oil

1 Cut pork into cubes, season with salt and pepper and dredge with flour.
2 Dip into egg and deep fry in oil for 4–5 minutes.
3 Heat sweet sour sauce.
4 Add pickled onions and the pork to it, and cook together for 1 minute.
5 Sprinkle with sesame oil, cook for ½ minute and serve.

Sweet and sour pork special

cooking time   7–10 minutes

you will need for 6 servings:

2 dozen egg noodle	4 oz. breast of chicken
squares	2 oz. pork, minced
3 oz. fresh pork	salt
4 oz. roast lean pork	2 oz. mushrooms, sliced
2 oz. fresh cucumber	2 oz. fresh prawns,
2 oz. celery	shelled
2 oz. onions	oil for deep frying
2 oz. water chestnuts	sweet sour sauce
2 oz. bamboo shoots	(see page 23)

1 Prepare egg noodle squares, using pastry described in recipe for Chinese Wun Tun Soup (see page 16).
2 Cut fresh pork, roast pork, cucumber, celery, onions, water chestnuts, bamboo shoots and breast of chicken very finely.
3 Roll a little of the minced pork and enclose it in one corner of each egg noodle square.
4 Heat an oiled pan and fry fresh pork in it for 1 minute. Season with salt.
5 Add roast pork, onions, bamboo shoots, cucumber, celery, water chestnuts, mushrooms, prawns and chicken.
6 Cook for 3 minutes.
7 Deep fry the egg noodle squares in plenty of oil for 2 minutes and arrange them on a dish.
8 Pour the sweet sour sauce over roast pork, vegetables, etc., cook for 1 minute.
9 Heap the contents of the pan on top of the egg noodle squares and serve.

Sweet and sour spare ribs

cooking time   about 1 hour

you will need for 6 servings:

2½ lb. spare ribs, cut	1 tablespoon Chinese
in 1-inch lengths	wine (or sherry)
1¼ pints water	2 sweet peppers, shredded
4 tablespoons soya sauce	2 tablespoons Chinese
1 teaspoon salt	sweet pickles
3½ tablespoons sugar	3 tablespoons vinegar
	2 tablespoons cornflour

1 Cut the ribs as described in recipe for Spare ribs (page 26). Put in a pan with 1 pint water soya sauce and salt. Bring to the boil, then simmer for 45 minutes.
2 Pour ribs and their gravy into a large frying pan, add half a tablespoon sugar and wine.
3 Stir over a high flame to coat all pieces with gravy and evaporate the liquid, for 6–7 minutes.
4 Add peppers and pickles, cook for 2 minutes, stirring all the time.
5 Mix remaining sugar with vinegar and cornflour, dilute with ¼ pint cold water, blend the mixture into the pan. Continue to cook, stirring all the time for 2–3 minutes and serve.

Spare ribs

cooking time   about 1 hour

you will need for 6 servings:

2 lb. pork spare ribs,	3 tablespoons soya sauce
chopped into 1-inch	1 teaspoon sugar
lengths	2 tablespoons Chinese
¾ pint water	wine (or sherry)
1 teaspoon salt	

1 Rinse and dry the ribs, cut into separate pieces, so that each little bone has some flesh.
2 Put into a pan, add water, salt and soya sauce.
3 Bring to the boil, then simmer gently for 45 minutes.
4 Transfer pork with all its gravy into a frying pan, sprinkle with sugar and wine and stir over a high flame to evaporate the liquid.

Note:

The idea is to coat all pieces of rib with the dressing and to keep stirring until they look dry.

Variation

Spare ribs with pineapple
Proceed as above, but allow 2 tablespoons of sugar and instead of wine add 4 oz. shredded pineapple to the frying pan.

Roast pork

cooking time   20 minutes

you will need for 4 servings:

1 lb. pork, fairly fat	1 teaspoon salt
1 tablespoon soya sauce, light	1 dessertspoon sugar
½ tablespoon soya sauce, dark	1 dessertspoon brandy (Chinese, if possible)

1 Cut the pork into slices, at least ½-inch thick.
2 Combine all the ingredients and steep the slices of pork in the mixture.
3 Roast for 20 minutes in a hot oven.

Spiced pork chops

cooking time   3–4 minutes

you will need for 4 servings:

2 pork chops	salt and pepper
½ oz. Chinese spice (Ng Heung Fun)	flour
¼ oz. red cheese (Nam Yue)	oil for deep frying

1 Cut chops, bones and all, into 1-inch pieces and place in a deep dish.
2 Sprinkle with Chinese spice, red cheese, salt and pepper and mix well.
3 Dredge with flour and deep fry in boiling oil for 3–4 minutes.

Pigs' trotters with pickles

cooking time   2 hours 45 minutes

you will need for 4 servings:

2 cleaned pigs' trotters	3 tablespoons vinegar
2 oz. green ginger	1 tablespoon sugar
1 tablespoon black soya beans	Chinese pickled cucumbers, sliced (or sweet pickled onions, chopped)
2 pints water	

1 Chop trotters into uniform pieces about 1-inch square.
2 Brown them with the ginger in a pan without any fat.
3 Scald and crush black soya beans, add to trotters, stir, simmer for 5 minutes.
4 Add water and leave to simmer for 2½ hours.
5 Add vinegar and sugar, simmer for 10 minutes and serve either on a foundation of pickled cucumbers or garnished with sweet pickled onions.

Pork chops with dried olives

cooking time   25 minutes

you will need for 4 servings:

1 oz. dried olives (Lahm Gok)	1 teaspoon salt
1 oz. salted beans (Dow See)	1 dessertspoon soya sauce
	1 teaspoon sugar
12 oz.–1 lb. chops	veal (or chicken stock)
1 tablespoon oil	1 teaspoon cornflour
	2 tablespoons cold water
1 clove garlic, crushed	few drops sesame oil

1 Soak olives in water for 5 minutes, drain, add to beans and chop together finely.
2 Cut chops, bones and all, into 1-inch pieces.
3 Heat oil in pan, add garlic and bean and olive mixture and cook for 1 minute.
4 Add pork, salt, soya sauce and sugar.
5 Cook briskly for 1 minute, stirring constantly.
6 Add enough stock to cover and simmer gently for 15 minutes.
7 Thicken with cornflour diluted with water.
8 Sprinkle with sesame oil. Cook for 1 minute and serve.

Pork and broccoli

cooking time   15–16 minutes

you will need for 4 servings:

1½ lb. broccoli	pinch salt
8 oz. shoulder of pork	2 dessertspoons soya sauce
3 tablespoons oil	
½ teaspoon Ve-Tsin	1 dessertspoon sherry
½ clove garlic, crushed	½ pint water
1 teaspoon sugar	2 tablespoons cornflour

1 Wash and cut broccoli into 1½-inch chunks.
2 Cut the pork into 1-inch squares, ¼-inch thick.
3 Fry in oil with Ve-Tsin, garlic, sugar, salt, soya sauce and sherry, for 10 minutes.
4 Add broccoli and all but one tablespoon of the water, cook together for 3 minutes.
5 Blend cornflour with the last tablespoon of water, add to pan, stir, cook for a further 3 minutes, by which time the sauce should thicken, and serve.

Beef with mixed vegetables

cooking time	10 minutes

you will need for 3–4 servings:

8 oz. beef	salt and pepper
1½ oz. bamboo shoots	1 dessertspoon sugar
2 oz. water chestnuts	½ teaspoon sesame oil
2 oz. fresh mushrooms	1 dessertspoon sherry
½ oz. preserved parsnips	1 dessertspoon soya
½ oz. fresh ginger	sauce
½ oz. lily petals	1 teaspoon cornflour
	2 tablespoons cold water

1 Cut beef, vegetables, ginger and lily petals into small pieces.
2 Place the beef on a dish.
3 Mix other chopped ingredients together.
4 Add salt and pepper, sugar, sesame oil, sherry, sauce and cornflour diluted with water.
5 Mix well and put over the beef.
6 Place the dish in a pan of hot water and steam for 10 minutes.

Steamed minced beef

cooking time	20 minutes

you will need for 4 servings:

2 oz. cabbage	1 teaspoon sugar
2 slices green ginger	1 dessertspoon soya sauce
½ teaspoon salt	2 dessertspoons water
1 lb. beef (rump), minced	1 dessertspoon peanut oil

1 Chop the cabbage and cut the ginger into thin strips.
2 Mix all ingredients.
3 Spread over a plate in a ½-inch thick pancake and steam for 20 minutes.

Beef with lotus roots

cooking time	2 hours 15 minutes

you will need for 4 servings:

1 lb. beef	1 teaspoon thick sweet
1 clove garlic	sauce
1 oz. fresh ginger	1 small piece dried
1 tablespoon oil	orange peel
salt	2 teaspoons soya sauce
few drops aniseed	4 oz. dried lotus roots
	veal stock (or beef stock)

1 Cut beef into uniform pieces.
2 Pound garlic and ginger separately.
3 Put garlic in a hot oiled pan, cook for a few minutes and remove.
4 Place beef in pan, salt to taste and 'scramble' (i.e. cook quickly, stirring frequently) for 5 minutes.
5 Add aniseed, ginger, thick sweet sauce and orange peel. Simmer for 5 minutes.
6 Add soya sauce, lotus roots and sufficient stock to cover.
7 Simmer slowly for 2 hours.

Fried shredded beef with onions and green peppers

•cooking time	10 minutes

you will need for 4 servings:

12 oz. rump steak	salt
8 spring onions, chopped	1 tablespoon flour
1–2 cloves garlic, chopped	2 tablespoons soya sauce
1 tablespoon lard	2 tablespoons water
2 green peppers, seeded and diced	pinch brown sugar

1 Cut beef into very thin strips.
2 Fry onions and garlic in lard for 2 minutes. Add peppers, reduce heat, simmer gently for 5 minutes. Sprinkle with salt.
3 Add beef and fry, stirring constantly for 1–2 minutes, until it changes colour.
4 Blend flour with soya sauce, water and sugar, pour the mixture over the beef, stir, bring to the boil, simmer for 2 minutes and serve.

Fried beef with green ginger

cooking time	5–6 minutes

you will need for 4 servings:

1 lb beef	stock
2 oz. fresh ginger	1 dessertspoon sherry
1 tablespoon Chinese salt beans with sauce (Hahm Dow)	1 teaspoon sugar
	1 teaspoon cornflour
1 tablespoon oil	2 tablespoons cold water
salt	few drops sesame oil

1 Cut beef and ginger into thin slices.
2 Put salt beans with sauce in hot oiled pan.
3 Season with salt and scramble for half a minute.
4 Add beef and ginger and cook for 1 minute.
5 Add sufficient stock to cover and cook for 1½ minutes.
6 Add sherry, sugar, cornflour mixed with water and sesame oil.
7 Stir, cook for 2½ minutes and serve.

Fried beef with celery and cabbage

cooking time	7–8 minutes

you will need for 4 servings:

1 lb. steak	2 oz. cabbage
1 teaspoon cornflour	2 oz. oil
2 tablespoons water	1 dessertspoon soya
2 oz. celery	sauce
1 small onion	salt and pepper

1 Slice beef finely.
2 Dilute cornflour with water and mix with the meat.
3 Shred celery, onions and cabbage.
4 Fry in a little oil for 3 minutes and remove.
5 Fry meat briskly in the rest of the oil, stirring all the time until each piece is browned.

6 Add onion, celery, cabbage and soya sauce.
7 Season to taste.
8 Simmer, stirring constantly, for 2 minutes and serve.

Spiced beef

cooking time   2 hours 35 minutes

you will need for 4–6 servings:

1–1½ lb. stewing steak	2 pints water
salt	8 pieces Chinese aniseed
1 tablespoon soya sauce	(Bart Gok)
1 tablespoon brandy	1½ teaspoons cornflour
1 dessertspoon oil	

1 Cut the meat into uniform pieces and sprinkle with salt.
2 Mix this with half soya sauce and brandy.
3 Heat oil in pan and brown the meat lightly.
4 Add remainder of soya sauce and brandy mixed with water.
5 Add Chinese aniseed.
6 Bring to the boil and simmer gently for 2¼ hours.
7 Before serving, thicken with cornflour diluted with 2 tablespoons water.

Ribs of beef with black beans

cooking time   40 minutes

you will need for 6 servings:

1½ lb. ribs of beef	1 dessertspoon brandy
salt	2 cloves garlic, crushed
1 tablespoon black soya	1 dessertspoon oil
beans (Dow See)	¼ pint water
1 dessertspoon soya sauce	

1 Cut the ribs into largish pieces, say 2-inch by 1-inch.
2 Sprinkle with salt.
3 Wash the beans, place them in a bowl, add soya sauce, brandy and 1 clove garlic.
4 Mix, crushing with a fork.
5 Heat oil with remaining clove garlic in a pan and brown the ribs.
6 Add black beans and rest of ingredients, stirring briskly for 2 minutes.
7 Add water, boil fast for 5 minutes, then simmer for 30 minutes and serve.

Steak with oyster sauce

cooking time   5–6 minutes

you will need for 4 servings:

12 oz. rump steak	1 dessertspoon oil
1 knob green ginger	1 clove garlic, crushed
1 dessertspoon soya sauce	2 dessertspoons oyster
1 dessertspoon brandy	sauce
1 dessertspoon cornflour	¼ pint water
pinch salt	

1 Slice meat wafer thin and pound the ginger.
2 Mix meat with ginger, soya sauce, brandy, cornflour and salt.
3 Heat oil in pan with garlic until garlic browns.
4 Discard garlic.
5 Add meat, stirring very briskly for 2 minutes.
6 Add oyster sauce and continue to cook fast, stirring all the time, for a further minute.
7 Add water, cook for half a minute and serve.

Steamed beef with rice

cooking time   40 minutes

you will need for 4 servings:

1 lb. lean beef, minced	12 water chestnuts
2 oz. bamboo shoots	4 oz. mushrooms
1 oz. preserved parsnips	1 oz. ginger
few drops sesame oil	few drops brandy
1 teaspoon cornflour	1 teaspoon sugar
1 lb. rice	salt
1 dessertspoon soya sauce	1½ pints boiling water
4 eggs	

1 Combine all ingredients except rice, eggs and water.
2 Chop finely and season to taste.
3 Bring water to the boil, pour over rice and steam for 25–30 minutes.
4 Put beef mixture on top of rice, cover and steam for a further 7–8 minutes.
5 Break the eggs and slide neatly on top of the beef.
6 Steam with lid on until the whites set and serve.

Veal with water chestnuts

cooking time   5–6 minutes

you will need for 4 servings:

8 oz. veal fillet	1 tablespoon soya sauce
6 water chestnuts	1½ teaspoons cornflour
4 oz. mushrooms	3 tablespoons cold water
2 tablespoons lard	

1 Cut the veal, water chestnuts and mushrooms into thin slices.
2 Heat lard, fry veal for 2 minutes, stirring frequently.
3 Add water chestnuts and mushrooms. Fry, stirring, for 2 minutes.
4 Season with soya sauce.
5 Dilute cornflour in water, add to pan, stir to blend, simmer for 1–2 minutes to thicken the sauce and serve.

Fried veal and celery

cooking time   15 minutes

you will need for 4 servings:

8 oz. veal fillet	1 teaspoon cornflour
8 oz. celery	2 tablespoons water
6 spring onions	1 oz. oil
4 oz. mushrooms	1 teaspoon brandy
1 clove garlic	1 tablespoon soya sauce

1 Cut meat and vegetables into thin slices.
2 Mix cornflour with water and coat the meat with it.
3 Fry vegetables in half the oil for 5 minutes.
4 Add rest of oil and fry meat for 5 minutes.
5 Add rest of ingredients, cook together for 5 minutes, stirring all the time, and serve.

Fried veal with green peppers

cooking time   8–9 minutes

you will need for 4–6 servings:

¾ lb. raw veal, diced	2–3 tablespoons bamboo
pinch salt	shoots, sliced
1 teaspoon cornflour	1 tablespoon sweet soya
1 egg white, lightly	bean paste
beaten	1 tablespoon ordinary
2 teaspoons Chinese wine	soya bean paste
(or sherry)	pinch sugar
4 oz. lard	pinch Ve-Tsin
2 oz. mushrooms, sliced	½ teaspoon chestnut
2 green peppers, seeded,	powder (or cornflour)
diced	1–2 tablespoons stock
	(or water)

1 Mix veal with salt, cornflour, egg white and wine.
2 Heat lard and fry veal for 2 minutes, remove and leave aside.
3 In the same fat fry together, mushrooms, peppers and bamboo shoots for 2 minutes. Remove and put with veal.
4 In the same pan fry the sweet and ordinary soya bean pastes for 2–3 minutes. Add veal and the vegetables, sprinkle with sugar and Ve-Tsin.
5 Blend chestnut powder with stock, stir into the pan, cook for 1 minute and serve.

Braised beef with pimentos

cooking time   10 minutes

you will need for 4 servings:

1 lb. beef (rump)	1 teaspoon sugar
1 lb. green pimentos	1 dessertspoon soya
2 tablespoons oil	sauce
1 teaspoon salt	1 dessertspoon cornflour
¼ pint water	2 tablespoons water
2 cloves garlic, crushed	1 dessertspoon oyster
2 slices green ginger	sauce

1 Slice meat finely.
2 Wash pimentos, open, remove seeds and shred.

3 Heat 1 tablespoon oil, add ½ teaspoon salt, toss the pimentos for 1 minute.
4 Add half the water and simmer for 2 minutes.
5 Remove pimentos and place aside.
6 Heat remainder of oil, add garlic, salt and ginger.
7 Toss meat quickly until pale brown all over.
8 Add sugar, soya sauce and water.
9 Simmer for 3 minutes, add pimentos, cook for 1 minute.
10 Add cornflour mixed with water. Blend in oyster sauce and serve.

Kid with preserved fruit

cooking time   3 hours

you will need for 6 servings:

6 lb. kid (scrag end)	2 seeds cardamom
boiling water	1 tablespoon sugar
½ oz. dried mushrooms	salt and pepper
1 oz. Chinese preserved	
fruits	

1 Cut the meat into small uniform pieces.
2 Place in saucepan of boiling water and cook for 2 minutes.
3 Add mushrooms, preserved fruit, cardamom and sugar, making sure that there is enough water to cover the meat.
4 Steam under a lid for 3 hours.
5 Season with salt and pepper and serve.

Note:

In China, shredded sugar cane is used for this dish instead of sugar.

Liver with water chestnuts

cooking time   12 minutes

you will need for 4 servings:

12 oz. calf's liver	juice of ½ lemon
1 teaspoon cornflour	1 teaspoon brown sugar
2 tablespoons soya sauce	1 can water chestnuts
1 tablespoon Chinese	oil for frying
wine (or sherry)	1 onion, thinly sliced
	salt

1 Cut the liver into bite-size pieces.
2 Dilute cornflour with soya sauce, wine and lemon juice. Add sugar, stir well, pour the mixture over the liver and leave to stand for 25 minutes. Drain, but keep the marinade.
3 Slice the water chestnuts, cook them in their own liquid for 5 minutes.
4 Drain.
5 Heat oil and fry onion until transparent, add water chestnuts and cook together for 1 minute.
6 Move onion and water chestnuts to one side, and in the same pan fry liver for 2 minutes, stirring, to make sure it changes colour on all sides.

7 Add liquid in which the liver was steeped. Cook, stirring all the time, for 1–2 minutes, until the sauce thickens.

8 Transfer to a warmed serving dish, sprinkle with very fine dry salt and serve.

Fried liver

cooking time   6–8 minutes

you will need for 4 servings:

1 lb. liver	1 tablespoon oil
1 dessertspoon cornflour	1 small onion, sliced
1 clove garlic, pounded	4 oz. mushrooms, sliced
1 tablespoon brandy (optional)	1 dessertspoon soya sauce
	4 spring onions, chopped

1 Slice the liver and mix with cornflour and garlic.

2 Add brandy if desired, to improve flavour of meat.

3 Brown quickly in oil and add onions and mushrooms.

4 Cook till meat is uniformly brown, then add soya sauce and spring onions.

Liver and kidney with cucumber, Shanghai style

cooking time   8 minutes

you will need for 4–6 servings:

2 fresh cucumbers	1 teaspoon cornflour
salt	2 tablespoons soya sauce
1 oz. kidney, soaked and diced	juice of ½ lemon
2–3 tablespoons lard	
8 oz. calf's liver, sliced	

1 Peel and dice cucumbers, sprinkle with salt and leave to stand for 20 minutes.

2 Fry kidney in lard for 3 minutes, move to one side.

3 Add liver and fry until it changes colour — 1–2 minutes.

4 Drain cucumbers and add to kidney and liver. Fry for 2 minutes.

5 Blend cornflour with soya sauce and lemon juice, pour over the contents of the frying pan, stir for ½–1 minute, until the sauce thickens. Check seasoning. If necessary, add salt.

6 Transfer to a heated serving dish and serve at once.

Note:

Do not add salt during cooking, but just before serving.

Kidney and onion

cooking time   10–12 minutes

you will need for 4 servings:

12 oz. ox kidney	1 dessertspoon oil
1 dessertspoon soya sauce	1 clove garlic
1 dessertspoon brandy	¼ pint water
salt	pepper
1 large onion	

1 Trim the kidney, remove all membranes, and slice.

2 Mix with soya sauce, brandy and salt to taste.

3 Cut onion into thick rings.

4 Heat oil in pan with garlic, and brown kidneys quickly.

5 When the kidneys are almost cooked, add onion and stir.

6 As soon as the onions are cooked, add water, bring to the boil, simmer for 1 minute, season with pepper and serve.

Fried kidney

cooking time   7–8 minutes

you will need for 4 servings:

12 oz. kidney	1 oz. oil
1 dessertspoon cornflour	8 oz. celery, shredded
1 dessertspoon brandy	1 tablespoon soya sauce
pinch powdered ginger	4 spring onions, chopped

1 Trim kidney and cut into thin slices.

2 Mix with cornflour, brandy and ginger.

3 Fry in oil over a high flame for 5 minutes, stirring constantly.

4 Add celery, cook for 2 minutes.

5 Add soya sauce, sprinkle with onions, stir and serve at once.

Mutton with mixed vegetables

cooking time   7 minutes

you will need for 4 servings:

oil for deep frying	salt
½ oz. rice noodles (Mai Fun)	8 oz. lean mutton, diced
2 oz. bamboo shoots, sliced	pepper
	1 teaspoon soya sauce
1 oz. cucumber, sliced	1 teaspoon sugar
2 oz. onions, sliced	1 teaspoon cornflour
6 oz. Chinese white cabbage, sliced	2 tablespoons water
	few drops sesame oil
2 oz. mushrooms, sliced	stock

1 Bring oil to the boil and deep fry rice noodles for 2 minutes.

2 Remove and drain.

3 Toss bamboo shoots, cucumber, onions, white cabbage and mushrooms for 1 minute in a hot, oiled pan.

4 Season with salt to taste.

5 Add mutton, pepper to taste, soya sauce, and cook, stirring constantly, for 2 minutes.

6 Add sugar, cornflour diluted with water, sesame oil and stock.

7 Cook for 2 minutes. Transfer to a serving dish and serve garnished with rice noodles.

Stewed mutton

cooking time   2 hours

you will need for 6–8 servings:

2 lb. leg of mutton	1 oz. dried orange peel
2 pints water	1 dessertspoon soya
1 tablespoon brandy	sauce
pinch powdered ginger	1 teaspoon salt

1 Cut meat into neat cubes.
2 Simmer in water, with lid on, on low heat for 2 hours, with brandy, ginger and orange peel.
3 Stir from time to time.
4 Season with soya sauce and salt, and serve.

Diced lamb with mixed vegetables

cooking time   35 minutes

you will need for 8–10 servings:

4 tablespoons oil	2 tablespoons treacle
2½ teaspoons salt	1½ pints boiling stock
½ teaspoon pepper	2 oz. fresh bean sprouts
1½ lb. lamb, as lean as possible, cut in 1-inch dice	4 oz. water chestnuts, sliced
3 tablespoons soya sauce	4 oz. fresh mushrooms, sliced
6 oz. celery, diced to match lamb	8 oz. Chinese cabbage, diced
6 oz. onion, diced	5 tablespoons cornflour
8 oz. green pimento, diced	¼ pint cold water
12 oz. French beans, diced	1 tablespoon roasted almonds

1 Heat oil with salt and pepper in a big heavy pan.
2 Toss the lamb in it for 5 minutes, to sear all sides.
3 Add soya sauce, stir, put in celery, onion, green pimento and beans. Stir.
4 Mix treacle with stock and add to pan, blending well.
5 Cover the pan and simmer gently for 15 minutes.
6 Add bean sprouts, water chestnuts, mushrooms and Chinese cabbage. Mix.
7 Cover and simmer for another 10 minutes.
8 Blend cornflour with cold water, stir into the pan.
9 Cook stirring constantly until sauce thickens (2–3 minutes).
10 Transfer to heated serving dish, sprinkle with almonds and serve at once.

Spiced leg of lamb

cooking time   3½ hours

you will need for 8–10 servings:

3–4 lb. leg of lamb	1 knob green ginger
salt	2 cloves garlic
water	10 pieces Chinese aniseed
1 tablespoon soya sauce	1½ pints stock
1 tablespoon brandy	cornflour (optional)
3 tablespoons oil	

1 Rub lamb with salt and boil in saucepan with enough water to cover, for 15 minutes.
2 Remove lamb from stock and put in a deep dish.
3 Allow to cool, then sprinkle with salt and rub with mixture of soya sauce and brandy.
4 Heat oil with ginger and garlic in pan big enough to take the leg of lamb.
5 Fry lamb in this mixture.
6 When it is nicely browned on all sides, add 1½ pints stock and any of the juice left in the dish and pour over the meat.
7 Add aniseed, bring to the boil and simmer gently for 2½–3 hours.

Note:

If desired, the sauce can be thickened with cornflour.

K'ao Yang jou
(Barbecued lamb, Peking style)

cooking time   8–10 minutes

you will need for 6 servings:

1½ lb. lean lamb	2 teaspoons sugar
3 tablespoons soya sauce	1 teaspoon salt
2 cloves garlic, crushed	

1 Cut the lamb into small thin slices.
2 Combine soya sauce, garlic, sugar and salt in a bowl. Add lamb and stir well to coat all slices with dressing. Leave to macerate for 15 minutes.
3 Just before serving, take slices of lamb out of the dressing, grill for 4–5 minutes on each side, using a charcoal burner if possible, and serve.

Lamb with bean sprouts

cooking time   10 minutes

you will need for 6 servings:

4 tablespoons oil	1 lb. lean lamb, cut in thin slices
½ clove garlic, crushed	
1 teaspoon salt	½ teaspoon sugar
½ teaspoon pepper	4 oz. bean sprouts
4 tablespoons soya sauce	3 tablespoons cornflour
1 teaspoon ginger root, crushed	2 tablespoons cold water
	3 spring onions, cut in 1½-inch pieces

1 Heat the oil with garlic, salt, pepper, soya sauce and ginger.
2 Sauté the lamb in this mixture for 5 minutes.
3 Cover and cook for 1 minute. Sprinkle in sugar.
4 Add bean sprouts, bring up the heat, mix and cook together for 3 minutes.
5 Blend cornflour with water, pour into the pan and simmer until the sauce thickens.
6 Sprinkle with spring onions and serve.

Fried lamb

cooking time   1 hour

you will need for 6 servings:

1½ lb. lamb (breast)	2 cloves garlic
salt	1 tablespoon soya sauce
water	1 tablespoon brandy
8 pieces Chinese aniseed	oil for deep frying
(Bart Gok)	

1 Rub lamb with salt and boil in enough water to cover it, adding aniseed and garlic.
2 When lamb is tender, allow to cool in its own stock.
3 Drain and cut into uniform pieces, say 2-inches by 1-inch.
4 Sprinkle with salt and soya sauce mixed with brandy and deep fry in smoking oil until crisp.
5 Serve at once.

Note:

This is an ideal way of using up left-overs of cold boiled lamb or mutton.

Lamb and Chinese vermicelli

cooking time   20 minutes

you will need for 4 servings:

8 oz. lamb	1 dessertspoon soya
1 teaspoon cornflour	sauce
2 tablespoons water	1 teaspoon brandy
4 oz. Chinese vermicelli	4 spring onions, chopped
2 tomatoes	1 teaspoon powdered
1 oz. oil	ginger

1 Cut meat into strips and mix with cornflour diluted with water.
2 Soak vermicelli in hot water for 5 minutes.
3 Peel and slice tomatoes.
4 Fry lamb quickly in hot oil for 5 minutes.
5 Add drained vermicelli and cook together.
6 Add soya sauce, brandy, spring onions, ginger and tomatoes and cook briskly for 5 minutes.
7 Add ½ pint water, simmer for 5 minutes and serve.

Variation

Lamb with turnips

As in previous recipe, replacing vermicelli by 8 oz. Chinese turnips shredded and reducing the amount of water added to the pan to ¼ pint.

Chicken with celery and mushrooms

cooking time   10 minutes

you will need for 6 servings:

1 lb. raw chicken meat,	1 tablespoon soya sauce
boned	1 tablespoon cornflour
1 head celery	4 tablespoons stock
2 tablespoons lard	(or cold water)
2–3 oz. mushrooms, sliced	

1 Cut chicken meat into thin slices.
2 String and cut celery into bite-size chunks.
3 Fry chicken in lard for 5 minutes, stirring all the time.
4 Add celery and mushrooms, stir, season with soya sauce.
5 Cook, stirring frequently for 3 minutes.
6 Dilute cornflour with stock, blend into the pan.
7 Simmer for 2 minutes and serve.

Stewed chicken with chestnuts

cooking time   1 hour 10 minutes

you will need for 6–8 servings:

1 chicken (1½–2 lb.)	1 oz. mushrooms (dried)
2 tablespoons gin	1 oz. Chinese preserved
small piece ginger,	fruits (Hung Jo)
minced or finely chopped	chicken (or veal stock)
1 clove garlic	8 oz. chestnuts, shelled
1 tablespoon oil	and skinned
salt	1 dessertspoon soya sauce
1 teaspoon sugar	few drops sesame oil

1 Cut chicken into neat slices about 1½-inches by ½-inch.
2 Combine gin and ginger and squeeze through muslin bag to extract all juice.
3 Cook garlic in hot oiled pan for ½ minute and remove.
4 Sprinkle pan with little salt, add chicken and cook for 5 minutes.
5 Add sugar and simmer for 2 minutes, stirring constantly.
6 Add gin and ginger juice, mushrooms (whole if small, halved if big) and Chinese preserved fruits.
7 Add enough stock to cover and simmer gently for 45 minutes, or longer if chicken is tough.
8 Add chestnuts and cook together for 10 minutes.
9 Sprinkle in soya sauce, sesame oil and serve.

Fried chicken with pineapple

cooking time   3 minutes

you will need for 4 servings:

8 oz. chicken, boned	1 teaspoon cornflour
1 big fresh pineapple	2 tablespoons water
(or 1 lb. canned pineapple)	sesame oil
oil	1 teaspoon brandy
salt	1 dessertspoon soya sauce
veal stock (or chicken	1 teaspoon sugar
stock)	

1 Cut chicken into thin slices and the pineapple into small cubes.
2 Heat a little oil in the pan, add pineapple.
3 Season with salt, add enough veal stock to cover and cook for 1 minute.
4 Add chicken, cornflour diluted with water, sesame oil, brandy, soya sauce and sugar.
5 Cook for 2 minutes and serve.

Fried chicken and mushrooms

cooking time   5 minutes

you will need for 4 servings:

breast of chicken	8 oz. cabbage
1 tablespoon cornflour	1 oz. oil
salt	1 dessertspoon soya sauce
1 dessertspoon brandy	3–4 spring onions,
8 oz. fresh mushrooms	chopped

1 Slice the breast of chicken into thin slices.
2 Mix with cornflour, little salt and brandy.
3 Slice mushrooms and cabbage and fry them in oil for 2 minutes.
4 Add chicken and scramble for 3 minutes, by which time every slice of chicken should be white.
5 Add soya sauce and spring onions and serve.

Chicken strips in oyster sauce

cooking time   25–30 minutes

you will need for 6 servings:

1 lb. chicken, boned	1 oz. bundle chives
2 teaspoons cornflour	$\frac{1}{4}$ oz. fresh ginger
$\frac{1}{2}$ teaspoon sugar	6 spring onions
1 teaspoon soya sauce	1 tablespoon peanut oil
pinch salt	1 tablespoon oyster sauce
3 oz. bamboo shoots	2 tablespoons water

1 Cut chicken meat into thin strips. Put in a bowl, sprinkle with 1 teaspoon cornflour, sugar, soya sauce and salt and mix well. Leave.
2 Bring bamboo shoots to the boil in enough salted water to cover, lower heat, simmer for 15 minutes, drain and cut to match the chicken.
3 Cut chives into 1-inch lengths.
4 Chop ginger and onions together very finely.
5 Toss bamboo shoots in a frying pan without any grease, to dry them off. Shake the pan and stir to prevent burning.
6 Heat oil in pan, add ginger and onion and fry for 2 minutes.
7 Add chicken and fry, stirring all the time, for 2 minutes.
8 Add bamboo shoots, stir carefully, cook for 1 minute.
9 Sprinkle in chives and blend in oyster sauce.
10 Dilute remaining cornflour with water, stir into the pan, cook for 1 minute to thicken the sauce and serve.

Fried spiced chicken

cooking time   7–8 minutes

you will need for 6–8 servings:

1 chicken (3$\frac{1}{2}$–4 lb.)	$\frac{1}{4}$ teaspoon pepper
$\frac{1}{2}$ teaspoon salt	1 tablespoon gin
$\frac{1}{2}$ teaspoon Chinese spice	oil for deep frying
(Ng Heung Fun)	

1 Cut chicken into quarters, and put into a basin.
2 Sprinkle with salt, Chinese spice, pepper and gin. Leave to macerate for 12 hours.
3 Drain the chicken and deep fry in a pan of boiling oil until it acquires a golden colour.
4 Drain. Cut into pieces 1-inch by $\frac{1}{2}$-inch.
5 Arrange on a dish, sprinkle with spices remaining on dish on which chicken was macerated, and serve.

Fried chicken with mixed vegetables

cooking time   4 minutes

you will need for 4 servings:

oil	soya sauce
2 oz. onions, chopped	chicken stock
2 oz. water chestnuts,	4 oz. breast of chicken,
sliced	sliced
2 oz. mushrooms, sliced	1 teaspoon cornflour
2 oz. celery, sliced	2 tablespoons cold water
2 oz. cucumber, sliced	$\frac{1}{2}$ teaspoon sesame oil
salt	1 teaspoon roasted
sugar	almonds, ground

1 Heat pan with sufficient oil to grease it.
2 Put in all vegetables and cook for 1 minute.
3 Add salt and sugar to taste, a little soya sauce and enough stock to cover.
4 Simmer with lid on for 1 minute.
5 Add chicken, cornflour diluted with water, and sesame oil.
6 Cook for 2 minutes.
7 Transfer to a serving dish, sprinkle with almonds and serve.

Stewed chicken with almonds

cooking time   4–5 minutes

you will need for 4 servings:

6 oz. chicken meat	1 teaspoon sugar
4 oz. roasted almonds	pepper
8 oz. onions	chicken (or veal stock)
3 oz. bamboo shoots	1 teaspoon cornflour
1 oz. mushrooms	2 tablespoons water
oil	few drops sesame oil
salt	1 teaspoon sherry

1 Dice the chicken, almonds, onions, bamboo shoots and mushrooms.
2 Heat pan with enough oil to grease it.
3 Put in bamboo shoots, onions and mushrooms.
4 Season with salt to taste and cook briskly for 1 minute.
5 Add sugar, a little pepper and enough stock to cover. Cook for 1 minute.
6 Add chicken, cornflour diluted with water, sesame oil and sherry.
7 Fry for 1 minute. Add almonds, fry for 1 minute and serve.

Fried chicken with rice noodles and mixed vegetables

cooking time   5 minutes

you will need for 4 servings:

hot water	2 oz. water chestnuts,
6 oz. thick rice noodles	sliced
4 oz. breast of chicken	2 oz. cucumber, sliced
oil	3 oz. bean sprouts
salt	½ oz. lichen (Wun Yee)
1 oz. onion, sliced	1 oz. button mushrooms
1 oz. celery, sliced	1 teaspoon sugar
2 oz. bamboo shoots,	1 teaspoon soya sauce
sliced	chicken stock

1 Pour hot water on the rice noodles and leave to stand for 20–25 minutes. Drain.
2 Slice the chicken and toss in a hot, oiled pan for 1 minute.
3 Season with salt to taste.
4 Add all the vegetables and the mushrooms.
5 Cook for 1 minute, then add sugar, soya sauce and enough stock to cover.
6 Cook for 1 minute, add noodles.
7 Cook for 2 minutes and serve.

Fried chicken giblets

cooking time   12 minutes

you will need for 4 servings:

1 lb. chicken giblets	1 medium-sized onion,
2 teaspoons cornflour	sliced
1 dessertspoon brandy	2 oz. white cabbage,
2 tablespoons oil	shredded
2 oz. mushrooms, sliced	1 dessertspoon soya sauce

1 Clean giblets, slice and mix with cornflour and brandy.
2 Using half the oil, fry mushrooms, onions and cabbage for 4 minutes.
3 Remove and keep hot.
4 Using the rest of the oil, fry the giblets for 5 minutes.
5 Season with soya sauce, add vegetables, stir, cook for 3 minutes and serve.

Variations

Fried giblets with bean sprouts
As in previous recipe, substituting 8 oz. bean sprouts for the cabbage.

Fried giblets with bamboo shoots
As above, substituting 8 oz. bamboo shoots for the bean sprouts.

Fried giblets with peas
As above, substituting 8 oz. peas (or small packet frozen peas) for bamboo shoots.

Fried giblets with broccoli
As above, substituting 1 large packet frozen broccoli, (or equivalent amount of fresh broccoli) for peas.

Fried giblets with mixed vegetables
As above, substituting 4 oz. French beans, 3–4 stalks of celery and ½ small cauliflower divided into flowerets, for broccoli.

Chicken livers with prawns and broccoli

cooking time   10–12 minutes

you will need for 4 servings:

1 packet frozen broccoli	1 oz. spring onions,
salted water	finely chopped
8 oz. chicken livers,	pepper
sliced	2 oz. fresh mushrooms,
cornflour	sliced
2 tablespoons lard	6 oz. prawns, peeled
salt	1 tablespoon soya sauce
¼ oz. fresh ginger,	pinch Ve-Tsin
finely chopped	

1 Boil the broccoli in a little salted water for 4 minutes and drain.
2 Roll chicken livers in cornflour lightly and brown for 1 minute in 1 tablespoon lard. Remove from heat, season with salt, sprinkle with ginger, spring onions and pepper.
3 Heat remaining tablespoon of oil, toss the mushrooms in it for 2 minutes. Add broccoli and cook together for 2 minutes.
4 Add liver with all its seasoning and prawns. Cook for 1 minute.
5 Mix teaspoon of cornflour with soya sauce and Ve-Tsin, dilute with 4 tablespoons water, blend into the pan. Cook for 1 minute and serve.

Chicken livers with almonds

cooking time   9 minutes

you will need for 4 servings:

4 chicken livers	½ teaspoon sugar
6 canned water chestnuts	¼ pint chicken stock (or
3 tablespoons oil	water with a bouillon
1 small onion, thinly	cube)
sliced	1 teaspoon cornflour
3 tablespoons bamboo	2–3 tablespoons cold
shoots, sliced	water
1 teaspoon soya sauce	2 oz. whole almonds,
½ teaspoon salt	blanched, roasted
½ teaspoon Ve-Tsin	

1 Bring the livers to the boil in enough salted water to cover, cook for 3 minutes, drain, cool and slice.
2 Slice the water chestnuts thinly.
3 Heat oil, fry onion for 1 minute.
4 Add chicken livers, water chestnuts and bamboo shoots. Cook for 1 minute.
5 Season with soya sauce, salt, Ve-Tsin and sugar. Moisten with stock, stir. Cook for 2 minutes.
6 Dilute cornflour with cold water, stir into the pan, cook for 1 minute.
7 Add almonds, cook together for 1 minute and serve.

Fried jointed chicken

cooking time   30–35 minutes

you will need for 8 servings:

1 roasting (or young boiling) fowl	1 oz. spring onions pepper and salt
1 lb. lard (or equivalent amount oil)	

1 Joint the chicken into eight pieces (if boiling fowl used, simmer for 30 minutes, allow to cool, then joint).
2 Heat fat and deep fry chicken until golden, allowing about 30 minutes, (or more if old bird used).
3 Make sure all pieces are well basted during cooking.
4 Drain on greaseproof paper and garnish with spring onions cut into 2-inch strips.
5 Mix salt and pepper in equal proportions, dry off slightly in the oven.
6 Sprinkle on chicken, and serve.

Fried chicken with bitter melon

cooking time $6\frac{1}{2}$ minutes

you will need for 4 servings:

8 oz. breast of chicken	salt
1 can bitter melon (or cucumber and green pepper)	veal (or chicken stock)
	1 dessertspoon sherry
	few drops sesame oil
1 dessertspoon oil for cooking	1 teaspoon cornflour
	2 tablespoons water
1 teaspoon garlic, crushed	1 teaspoon sugar
1 teaspoon black bean paste	1 teaspoon soya sauce

1 Cut chicken and bitter melon into very thin strips.
2 Heat oil in pan, put in garlic, black bean paste and a pinch of salt and scramble for $\frac{1}{2}$ minute.
3 Add bitter melon, cook for 1 minute.
4 Cover with stock.
5 Simmer for 2 minutes, then add chicken, sherry, sesame oil and cornflour diluted with water.
6 Simmer for 2 minutes.
7 Add sugar and soya sauce.
8 Cook for 1 minute and serve.

Chicken in white cloud

cooking time   45–50 minutes

you will need for 6–8 servings:

1 young oven-ready chicken (about 3 lb.)	1 tablespoon dark soya sauce
salt	1 tablespoon honey
3 cloves garlic	prawn crackers
3–4 leeks	(see page 63)
2 tablespoons sherry	

1 Rub chicken with salt.
2 Crush garlic and cut leeks into 2-inch chunks. Sprinkle with 1 teaspoon sherry and soya sauce and use for stuffing the chicken.

3 Stitch up the opening.
4 Mix remaining sherry, soya sauce and honey, rub into the chicken and leave for 15 minutes to absorb the dressing.
5 Heat oven (375°F.–Gas Mark 4).
6 Brush the chicken with the dressing again and put to bake.
7 Turn from time to time as one side browns, painting the side you want to brown with the sherry-soya-honey mixture. Cook for 45–50 minutes.
8 Remove from oven, cut up, arrange on a heated serving dish giving the bird as near its original shape as you can achieve, cover with freshly made prawn crackers (to make the 'white cloud') and serve.

Sweet and sour chicken with pineapple

cooking time   6–7 minutes

you will need for 6 servings:

1 lb. chicken, boned and diced	1 dessertspoon peanut oil
	$\frac{1}{4}$ pint water
2 teaspoons salt	$\frac{1}{4}$ pint vinegar
1 teaspoon sugar	4 oz. sugar for sauce
1 dessertspoon soya sauce	8 oz. pineapple, diced
3 tablespoons plain flour	1 dessertspoon cornflour
2 eggs, beaten	2 tablespoons water
oil for deep frying	

1 Sprinkle chicken with 1 teaspoon salt, sugar and soya sauce, mix well and coat with plain flour.
2 Dip chicken pieces into egg and deep fry in smoking hot oil until golden. (This should not take more than $2\frac{1}{4}$–3 minutes.)
3 Strain and keep hot.
4 Heat peanut oil in a saucepan, add water, vinegar and the remaining salt and sugar.
5 Bring to the boil, add pineapple, and cornflour mixed with water, remove from heat.
6 Add chicken, mix well and serve at once.

Sweet and sour chicken

cooking time   5 minutes

you will need for 4 servings:

$\frac{1}{4}$ chicken, boned	1 dessertspoon oil
salt	sweet sour sauce
cornflour	(see page 60)
1 egg, beaten	

1 Shred the chicken, sprinkle with salt.
2 Spread cornflour on a sheet of greaseproof paper.
3 Dip chicken in egg and cornflour.
4 Heat oil in pan and fry the chicken briskly for 2 minutes, stirring constantly.
5 Add sweet sour sauce, stir, simmer for 3 minutes and serve.

Lemon-flavoured chicken

cooking time   30 minutes

you will need for 6 servings:

1 tender, drawn chicken	1 tablespoon sugar
1 tablespoon dark soya sauce	1 teaspoon Ve-Tsin
1 lemon, cut in thin slices	½ pint chicken stock (or water with a bouillon cube)
1 tablespoon Chinese wine (or sherry)	

1 Brush the chicken with soya sauce.
2 Sprinkle lemon slices with wine, sugar and Ve-Tsin, mix well and cover the chicken with them, spooning over any left-over dressing.
3 Put in an ovenproof dish, add stock, cover and cook in a hot oven (425°F.–Gas Mark 6) for 30 minutes.
4 Remove, chop into pieces, arrange on a heated serving dish and serve with its own gravy poured over the chicken.

Silver and jade chicken

cooking time   7–8 minutes

you will need for 6 servings:

1 large packet frozen broccoli	1 teaspoon cornflour
¾ lb. cooked chicken breast, boned	½ teaspoon salt
4 oz. ham, sliced	1 tablespoon peanut oil
pinch Ve-Tsin	½ pint chicken stock (or water with a bouillon cube)

1 Boil broccoli in salted water for 6 minutes and drain.
2 Cut chicken into thin slices. Put a slice of ham between two slices of chicken and sandwich together.
3 Arrange these chicken and ham 'sandwiches' on a dish.
4 Garnish with broccoli stalks, cut into 1½-inch lengths.
5 Combine Ve-Tsin, cornflour and salt. Heat oil and fry the Ve-Tsin mixture for a few seconds.
6 Dilute with stock, adding it little by little and blending in smoothly. Simmer for 1 minute, pour over the Silver and Jade Chicken and serve.

Chicken wings stuffed with ham and mushrooms

cooking time   45–50 minutes

you will need for 4 servings:

8 chicken wings, without feathers	1 teaspoon gin
16 pieces each ham, lean pork and mushrooms in strips 2-inches long	1 teaspoon cornflour
	2 tablespoons water
	few drops sesame oil
chicken (or veal stock)	few drops soya sauce
salt	1 teaspoon sherry

1 Cut each wing into two and take out bones without breaking skin.
2 Put 1 piece of ham, pork and mushroom in each half.
3 Place in a dish, add sufficient stock to cover, season with salt to taste and sprinkle with gin.
4 Steam until wings are tender.
5 Strain off stock.
6 Arrange wings on a serving dish.
7 Add to stock, cornflour diluted with water, sesame oil, soya sauce and sherry.
8 Bring to boil, stir, pour over wings and serve at once.

Steamed chicken wings and legs

cooking time   1 hour

you will need for 4 servings:

wings and legs of 1 chicken	1 dessertspoon cornflour
1 tablespoon soya sauce	4 oz. mushrooms, sliced
	salt and pepper

1 Chop wings and legs into small pieces, including bones.
2 Mix with soya sauce and cornflour.
3 Add mushrooms. Season with salt and pepper.
4 Place in a deep dish and steam for 1 hour.

Velvet chicken

cooking time   30–35 minutes

you will need for 6 servings:

1 tender chicken	4 oz. mushrooms, sliced
6 tablespoons cornflour	4 pints boiling water
¼ pint cold water	1 teaspoon salt
2 whites of egg, beaten lightly	½ teaspoon pepper
1 lb. fresh (or frozen) peas	1 tablespoon soya sauce

1 Skin the chicken, take the flesh off the bones and cut into uniform pieces.
2 Mix half cornflour with half the cold water and white of egg.
3 Use this mixture to coat the chicken pieces and leave for 10–15 minutes, then drop them one at a time into boiling water. (The water must not be allowed to come off the boil.)
4 Parboil the chicken quickly, 2–3 minutes, remove with perforated spoon, rinse under a cold water tap and drain.
5 Put the peas and mushrooms together in ½ pint boiling water.
6 Allow to come to the boil again, then cook for 3–4 minutes.
7 Add chicken, salt and pepper, cover the pan and simmer for 10 minutes.
8 Mix the rest of cornflour with 2 tablespoons cold water and blend into the pan.
9 Cook until the sauce thickens, add soya sauce, stir and serve.

Steamed chicken

cooking time   5–6 hours

you will need for 4–6 servings:

1 boiling fowl   pepper
4 pints water   pinch powdered ginger
1 teaspoon salt

1 Put fowl in basin big enough to contain it and the water.
2 Add water, salt, pepper and ginger.
3 Stand basin in steamer and steam slowly for 5–6 hours.

Note:

Chicken cooked this way keeps all its flavour.

Chinese chicken kromeskis

cooking time   7–8 minutes

you will need for 4–6 servings:

1 lb. breast of chicken,   2 tablespoons cornflour
  skinned   ¼ pint water
4 oz. lean ham; sliced   1 egg
2 oz. bamboo shoots   salt
1 oz. spring onions   2 tablespoons oil
2 oz. fresh mushrooms,   1 tablespoon oyster sauce
  sliced   1 dessertspoon brandy
1 dessertspoon soya sauce   pepper
1 tablespoon sherry

1 Cut chicken into uniform, oblong strips, about 3-inches by 1½-inches and about ⅛- inch thick.
2 Beat them slightly to flatten them but do not beat out of shape.
3 Cut ham into similarly shaped strips, 1½-inches long and ¼-inch wide.
4 Cut bamboo shoots to about the same size as the ham, and the spring onions into 1½-inch strips.
5 Cut mushrooms into thin strips.
6 Mix soya sauce, sherry and 1 dessertspoon cornflour with the water.
7 Whisk egg in a bowl. Lay rest of cornflour on a piece of greaseproof paper.
8 Lay chicken slices on a board, sprinkle with salt.
9 Place on each slice a strip of ham, on top of that a strip of bamboo shoot, then mushrooms, then spring onions.
10 Roll up the chicken and seal with the beaten egg.
11 Dip these little cigar-shaped rolls in egg, then into cornflour (a cocktail stick can be used for securing the rolls but this is considered cheating, and the sticks must, of course, be removed before serving).
12 Heat the oil and fry chicken rolls for 5 minutes, turning them gently until golden all over.
13 Add oyster sauce and cook for 2 minutes, stirring carefully, or shaking the pan from time to time to avoid damaging the rolls.

14 Add brandy, bring to the boil, season with pepper to taste, and serve.

Melting snowballs

cooking time   3 minutes

you will need for 6 servings:

8 oz. breast of chicken,   8 oz. lard
  raw   ¼ pint chicken stock
cold water   ½ tablespoon sherry
3 teaspoons cornflour   2 tablespoons ham,
1 teaspoon salt   minced and cooked
pinch sugar
½ teaspoon Ve-Tsin
4 egg whites, stiffly
  beaten

1 Mince the chicken meat and pound in a mortar into a fine paste, adding 2 tablespoons water gradually, to keep the mixture moist.
2 Add half the cornflour, and the salt, sugar, Ve-Tsin and 1 egg white. Stir, blend in 2 more tablespoons cold water into the mixture and gently fold in remainder of egg whites.
3 Heat lard without allowing it to boil hard.
4 Taking a teaspoonful of the chicken mixture at a time, drop into lard, fry for half a minute, turn to ensure uniform cooking, fry for another half minute, drain and keep warm.
5 Pour off all but 1 tablespoon of the fat in which the 'snowballs' were fried.
6 Dilute with stock and sherry.
7 Blend the remaining cornflour with 2 tablespoons cold water, stir into the pan, bring to the boil, simmer for half a minute, add 'snowballs', heat through and transfer to a heated serving dish.
8 Sprinkle with ham and serve.

Chicken with walnuts

cooking time   9–10 minutes

you will need for 4 servings:

4 oz. fresh mushrooms   1 dessertspoon oyster
8 oz. chicken, diced   sauce
1 dessertspoon soya sauce   2 oz. celery, diced
1 dessertspoon brandy   4 oz. walnuts, shelled
1 teaspoon cornflour   and skinned
salt   ¼ pint water
1 tablespoon oil   spring onions, chopped
1 clove garlic, crushed   (optional)

1 Cut mushrooms into ¼-inch strips.
2 Combine chicken with soya sauce, brandy, cornflour and salt to taste.
3 Heat oil in pan and brown garlic in it.
4 Remove garlic and sauté chicken briskly without allowing it to brown (2 minutes).
5 Add oyster sauce, mushrooms and celery. Simmer for 5 minutes, stirring constantly.
6 Add walnuts and water. Simmer for 2 minutes, and serve.

Note:

If desired, this dish can be garnished with chopped spring onions.

Variation

Chicken with almonds

Proceed as above, substituting blanched almonds for walnuts, but whereas the walnuts are added to the dish shortly before it is served, the almonds should be fried in an oiled pan with a little salt before adding. The frying of almonds requires great care as they tend to burn very quickly. They must be stirred constantly and removed as soon as they turn golden. Drain on greaseproof paper then add to dish as described above.

Crystal chicken

cooking time   3–3½ hours

you will need for 6 servings:

1 tender chicken	1 slice green ginger
3–4 metal spoons	2 spring onions
boiling water	2 small onions, sliced

1 Clean and draw the chicken and insert metal spoons into it to act as heat conductors.
2 Choose a saucepan large enough to hold both the bird and enough water to cover.
3 Measure out the required amount of water, bring it to the boil and add ginger, spring onions and onion. (This counteracts the oily taste of the skin.)
4 Put the chicken into the boiling water. Wait until boiling is re-established. Boil fast for 30 seconds.
5 Remove from heat, cover the saucepan and leave the chicken to get quite cold. This should take about 3–3½ hours.
6 When quite cold, drain the chicken, slice and serve with one of the following sauces:

Sauce No. 1

you will need for 6 servings:

1 tablespoon soya sauce	spring onions, few finely
1 tablespoon cooked	chopped
peanut oil	

1 Mix a tablespoon of soya sauce with a tablespoon of cooked peanut oil.
2 Add spring onions.

Sauce No. 2

you will need for 6 servings:

salt	spring onions, finely
2 tablespoons peanut oil	cut
1 teaspoon raw ginger,	
minced	

1 Mix a pinch of salt with peanut oil and ginger.
2 Add spring onions.

Chicken in salt

cooking time   1 hour 15 minutes

you will need for 6 servings:

1 roasting chicken	3–4 lb. salt
(3½–4 lb.), trussed	

1 Dry the chicken with a cloth inside and out.
2 Pour the salt into a pan deep enough to take all of it and the chicken.
3 Heat, until very hot, stirring frequently.
4 Make a well in the middle, put the chicken into it and cover with salt completely.
5 Cover the pan tightly (sealing with flour and water paste, if the cover does not fit well enough).
6 Cook over slow heat for 30 minutes, turn off heat, leave the chicken without opening the pan for another 30 minutes.
7 Take the chicken out of the salt, leave it to cool a little (about 15 minutes) and serve.

Chicken with tomatoes

cooking time   15–20 minutes

you will need for 4 servings:

½ chicken	teaspoon salt
1 pint water	1 teaspoon brandy
1 tablespoon oil	pepper
1 lb. tomatoes, peeled	
and quartered	

1 Cut chicken into uniform thin slices and simmer in water until the meat is tender.
2 Heat oil, toss tomatoes in it and add to the chicken.
3 Season with salt.
4 Add brandy and simmer for 10 minutes.
5 Add pepper and more salt if necessary and serve with plain boiled rice.

Deep fried whole chicken

cooking time   30–35 minutes

you will need for 4 servings:

1 young chicken	salt
1 lb. lard (or 1 pint oil)	

1 Wash and dry chicken on a cloth.
2 Heat lard and deep fry the chicken until it acquires a golden colour.
3 Baste chicken frequently inside and out.
4 Cook for about 30–35 minutes.
5 Drain, sprinkle with salt, and serve.

Note:

The chicken should be crisp outside and tender inside.

Spiced chicken wings with oyster sauce

cooking time   25 minutes

you will need for 4–8 servings:

8 chicken wings, trimmed and washed	4 teaspoons salt
1 pint boiling water	2 teaspoons sugar
juice ½ lemon	1 tablespoon powdered cinnamon
2 tablespoons soya sauce	½ tablespoon powdered ginger
2 tablespoons oyster sauce	¼ teaspoon pepper
½ pint chicken stock	

1 Put the chicken wings into a saucepan, add enough water to cover and the lemon juice. (The squeezed lemon may also be added.)
2 Bring to the boil, reduce heat, simmer for 5 minutes and drain.
3 Put in another pan, cover with mixed soya sauce, oyster sauce, stock, ½ teaspoon salt and sugar.
4 Bring to the boil, then simmer gently for 20 minutes. Drain and leave to cool.
5 Mix the rest of the salt with cinnamon, ginger and pepper in a small pan.
6 Heat this mixture, coat the wings with it and serve.

Braised chicken with pimentos

cooking time   9–10 minutes

you will need for 4 servings:

1 young chicken	2 slices green ginger
3–4 pimentos	½ teaspoon sugar
3 dessertspoons oil	1 dessertspoon sherry
1 teaspoon salt	1 dessertspoon cornflour
¼ pint water	1 dessertspoon soya sauce

1 Cut chicken into uniform pieces 1-inch by ½-inch, and dice the pimentos.
2 Heat oil in pan, add ½ teaspoon salt and quickly toss the pimentos in it for about 15 seconds, stirring constantly.
3 Add half the water and cook for 3 minutes.
4 Remove pan from heat.
5 In another pan, heat the rest of the oil and salt, add ginger and quick fry the chicken for 10 seconds, stirring constantly.
6 Add sugar, sherry and remainder of water. Simmer gently for 5 minutes (longer, if an old bird is used).
7 Add pimentos and their juice, cook for 30 seconds.
8 Add cornflour diluted with 2 tablespoons water and soya sauce. Stir and serve.

Variations

Braised duck with pimentos
Proceed as above, substituting duck for chicken.

Braised duck with courgettes
Proceed as above, substituting courgettes for pimentos.

Braised duck with cabbage
Proceed as above, substituting cabbage (if possible, Chinese white cabbage) for courgettes.

Braised duck with Brussels sprouts
Proceed as above, substituting Brussels sprouts for cabbage.

Braised duck with asparagus tips
Proceed as above, substituting asparagus tips for Brussels sprouts.

Braised duck with cauliflower
Proceed as above, substituting cauliflower for asparagus tips.

Braised duck with bean sprouts
Proceed as above, substituting bean sprouts for cauliflower.

Chicken Chow Min

cooking time   12–13 minutes

you will need for 6 servings:

6 oz. chicken, shredded	1 clove garlic, crushed
6 oz. lean pork, shredded	pepper
salt	1 dessertspoon oyster sauce
½ teaspoon Ve-Tsin	
1 teaspoon soya sauce	1 onion, sliced
1 teaspoon brandy (optional)	8 oz. cabbage, shredded
	4 oz. celery, diced
1 dessertspoon cornflour	2 tablespoons cold water
oil for cooking	½ oz. spring onions, chopped
1½ lb. noodles cooked	

1 Place chicken and pork in a bowl, add a little salt, Ve-Tsin, soya sauce, brandy, half the cornflour, and 1 teaspoon oil. Mix well.
2 Heat enough oil in pan to cover bottom of pan evenly, and fry noodles quickly (1–2 minutes). (They should be crisp on the outside and soft inside.)
3 Remove, drain and keep hot.
4 Heat 1 dessertspoon oil with the garlic and fry chicken and pork for 5 minutes.
5 Add oyster sauce, salt and pepper to taste, onion, cabbage and celery, and cook for 5 minutes.
6 Dilute remainder of cornflour with water, add to the pan, bring to the boil.
7 Stir, add spring onions. Pour mixture over noodles and serve.

Chicken and mushrooms

cooking time   6–7 minutes

you will need for 4 servings:

½ chicken	8 oz. fresh mushrooms
salt	2 cloves garlic, crushed
1 dessertspoon soya sauce	1 dessertspoon oyster sauce
1 dessertspoon brandy	
1 dessertspoon cornflour	½ pint water
1 knob green ginger, chopped	3–4 spring onions, chopped
1½ dessertspoons oil	

1 Bone the chicken, dice it and sprinkle with salt to taste.
2 Mix chicken with soya, brandy, cornflour, ginger and half teaspoon oil. Blend well.
3 Slice mushrooms.
4 Heat rest of oil in pan with garlic, allow garlic to brown, add chicken, stirring constantly until chicken is half cooked (2–3 minutes).
5 Add oyster sauce and mushrooms, stir, cook for 3 minutes.
6 Add water. Blend the sauce well.
7 Cook for 1 minute. Sprinkle with spring onions and serve.

Chicken with chestnuts

cooking time 1 hour 45 minutes

you will need for 4 servings:

½ small chicken
1 pint water
1 lb. chestnuts, peeled
1 tablespoon oil
2 tablespoons soya sauce

1 tablespoon cornflour
pepper
3–4 spring onions, chopped

1 Cut chicken into uniform pieces and cook slowly in water for 1 hour.
2 Add chestnuts, oil and soya sauce and simmer for 45 minutes.
3 Thicken with cornflour blended with 2 tablespoons water.
4 Season with pepper to taste, sprinkle with spring onions and serve.

Fairy duck

cooking time 4 hours

you will need for 6 servings:

1 fat duck
salt and pepper
2 tablespoons Chinese wine (or sherry)
1 teaspoon ginger, minced
3–4 spring onions, cut in 1½-inch lengths
3–4 slices fresh ginger

stock (or water)
2 oz. ham (Chinese, if possible), sliced cooked
2 oz. bamboo shoots, sliced
Wun-tun (or Chinese boiled patties) (page 17)

1 Clean duck, wash, dry on a cloth and rub with salt and pepper.
2 Mix wine with ginger, rub the mixture all over duck and leave to stand for 1 hour.
3 Put duck in a braising pan or an oven dish with a tightly fitting lid.
4 Add all its dressing, onions and ginger. Add enough light stock just to cover the bird.
5 Check seasoning, allowing both for dilution of the original dressing and for the salt content in the stock.

6 Bring to the boil, then cook gently either on a low heat or in a slow oven for 3 hours and 50 minutes.
7 Add ham cut into uniform-sized pieces and bamboo shoots. Cook for 10 minutes.
8 Serve with Wun-tun, cooked separately.

Braised duck with onions

cooking time 1 hour 15 minutes

you will need for 4–6 servings:

1 duck, singed and cleaned
1½ teaspoon salt
1½ lb. small pickling onions
1 dessertspoon soya sauce

1 dessertspoon brandy
1 clove garlic, crushed
2 tablespoons oil
1¼ pints water
1 teaspoon cornflour

1 Rub duck with salt and leave to stand while onions are being peeled.
2 Combine soya, brandy and garlic and rub duck with the mixture.
3 Heat oil in a pan and brown the duck all over, then add whole small onions.
4 Add water, cover with a lid, and cook in a moderate oven for 1 hour, basting frequently.
5 Add cornflour diluted with 2 tablespoons water to thicken the gravy.
6 Bring to the boil and serve.

Braised duck with lettuce

cooking time 1 hour 20 minutes

you will need for 6 servings:

1 duck, singed and cleaned
salt
2 dessertspoons soya sauce
1 teaspoon cinnamon

1 dessertspoon brandy
2 tablespoons oil
1½ pints water
1 teaspoon cornflour
1 large Cos lettuce

1 Sprinkle duck with 1 teaspoon salt.
2 Mix soya, cinnamon and brandy together and rub the mixture into the duck.
3 Heat oil in large pan and brown the duck thoroughly.
4 Add water, bring to the boil, reduce heat and simmer gently for 1 hour.
5 Add cornflour diluted with 2 tablespoons water, to thicken the sauce.
6 Shred lettuce, arrange it on a serving dish and use as foundation for the duck.
7 Reduce the pan juices, pour over the duck and serve.

Fragrant crisp duck

cooking time   2–2½ hours

you will need for 6 servings:

peanut (or other vegetable oil for deep frying)	12 oz. peeled shrimps, chopped (or prawns)
1 duck, (4 lb.) cleaned and drawn	4 oz. fat pork, diced
dark soya sauce	1 raw duck egg
2 tablespoons spring onions, chopped	Ve-Tsin
	salt
¼ pint chicken stock (or water)	cornflour
	1 egg, beaten

1 Heat the oil.
2 Open the duck by cutting along the back. Paint with soya sauce.
3 Deep fry in oil, using a frying basket, until brown and drain.
4 This operation helps to seal the skin. Line a pan just large enough to hold the duck with spring onions, lay the duck on top, add stock, cover and simmer gently for 1¼–1¾ hours until tender. Remove and carefully bone the duck through the opening along the back without breaking the skin.
5 Dice the duck meat, mix with shrimps and pork, bind with duck egg, season to taste with Ve-Tsin and salt, mix well and put the mixture into the duck skin. Carefully stitch up the opening.
6 Put oil to heat again.
7 Roll duck in cornflour, coat with beaten egg, lower into hot oil in frying basket and deep fry until pale golden. Drain, arrange on a heated serving platter and serve with liquid in which it was simmered during the second cooking operation, brought to the boil and strained, served separately.

Note:

This is a Szechuen speciality and well worth the trouble.

Duck stuffed with barley

cooking time   3 hours

you will need for 8–10 servings:

1 oz. lotus seeds	1 oz. fresh lean pork
water	1 duck (5 lb.)
2 oz. barley	1 small piece ginger
1 oz. mushrooms	1 tablespoon gin
1 oz. bamboo shoots	1 teaspoon salt
1 oz. water chestnuts	1 dessertspoon sugar
1 oz. ham	stock
1 oz. roast lean pork	

1 Soak lotus seeds in hot water for 30 minutes and skin.
2 Place in a saucepan, with double the amount of water required to cover, simmer for 1½ hours and strain.

3 Soak barley for 15 minutes. Add double the amount of water required for covering it.
4 Boil for 1 hour. Rinse under cold water tap and leave to drain.
5 Slice mushrooms, bamboo shoots, water chestnuts, ham, roast and fresh pork, or cut into dice.
6 Draw and bone duck through neck opening, taking care not to break the skin.
7 Pound the ginger, mix with gin and squeeze through a muslin bag to extract all juice.
8 Mix mushrooms, bamboo shoots, water chestnuts, ham and pork with the gin and ginger juices. Add salt and sugar, mix.
9 Add lotus seeds and barley and enough stock to bind the mixture. Use this mixture for stuffing the duck.
10 Sew up neck opening. Steam until tender.
11 Remove 'stitches'. Arrange on a dish. Garnish with shredded Chinese ham, and serve.

Variation

Duck stuffed with noodles

cooking time   1½ hours

Stuff duck with Braised noodles (see page 79), then proceed as above.

Braised duck stuffed with rice

cooking time   2 hours 20 minutes

you will need for 6 servings:

1 duck singed and cleaned	1 tablespoon Chinese wine (or Vermouth)
glutinous rice for stuffing	pepper and salt
4 pints water	1 oz. spring onions, chopped
¼ pint soya sauce	

1 Boil duck in enough water to cover for 30 minutes.
2 Stuff with glutinous rice and put to simmer in water on low heat for 45–50 minutes.
3 Pour off the water, leaving duck in pan.
4 Add soya sauce, vermouth and simmer for 1 hour, turning duck to brown all over.
5 Serve with salt, pepper and spring onions.

Duck and tangerine peel

cooking time   2½–3 hours

you will need for 6 servings:

1 duck, singed and cleaned	1 teaspoon powdered ginger
3 pints water	2–3 spring onions
2 oz. dried tangerine peel	salt and pepper

1 Simmer the duck slowly in water for 2½–3 hours until tender, together with all other ingredients, keeping the pan covered.
2 Serve, seasoned with salt and pepper.

Fivespice duck

cooking time   35—40 minutes

you will need for 6 servings:

1 pint soya sauce	1 duck, jointed
2 oz. sugar	oil for deep frying
1 tablespoon powdered	celery salt
cinnamon	3—4 spring onions,
1—2 aniseeds	chopped
1 pint water	

1 Mix soya sauce, sugar, cinnamon, aniseed and water in a deep narrow pan.
2 Bring to the boil and add the duck.
3 Reduce heat at once and simmer gently for 30 minutes.
4 Drain the duck pieces, wipe dry and deep fry until golden.
5 Drain, sprinkle with celery. salt and spring onions.

Steamed duck with mushrooms

cooking time   55 minutes

you will need for 4 servings:

1 duck (about 2 lb.)	1 clove garlic, crushed
oil for frying	2 oz. fresh mushrooms
salt and pepper	veal (or chicken stock)
1 tablespoon sherry	cornflour
1 dessertspoon soya sauce	2 tablespoons cold water
1 teaspoon sugar	few drops sesame oil

1 Cut duck in half, remove backbone, then cut duck in pieces about 1¼-inches by ½-inch.
2 Put duck in hot oiled pan with salt and pepper to taste, sherry, soya sauce and sugar.
3 Cook briskly for 3 minutes, stirring frequently.
4 Remove duck and leave on a plate.
5 Add a little more oil to pan and heat.
6 Add garlic and cook for ½ minute then remove garlic.
7 Cook mushrooms in same pan for 5 minutes, add the duck and enough stock to cover.
8 Simmer for 45 minutes, thicken with cornflour diluted with water.
9 Sprinkle in sesame oil. Cook for a further minute and serve.

Duck with black beans

cooking time   4—5 minutes

you will need for 4 servings:

4 oz. roast duck, diced	1 clove garlic, crushed
½ teaspoon salt	1 tablespoon onion,
pinch sugar	chopped
pinch Ve-Tsin	2 tablespoons peanut oil
few drops sesame oil	¼ pint chicken stock
1 teaspoon soya sauce	(or water with a
2 teaspoons cornflour	bouillon cube)
4 slices fresh ginger	1 tablespoon Chinese
2 tablespoons canned	wine (or sherry)
black beans	2 tablespoons cold water

1 Put duck meat in a bowl, sprinkle with salt, sugar, Ve-Tsin, sesame oil, soya sauce and 1 tablespoon cornflour. Mix well and leave to macerate for 5 minutes.
2 Chop the ginger with the beans, add garlic and pound together into a paste.
3 Fry onion in peanut oil for 1 minute, without allowing it to brown.
4 Add black bean paste and cook, stirring all the time, for 1 minute.
5 Add duck, stir, moisten with stock and wine. Cook for 1 minute.
6 Check seasoning, adding more salt or Ve-Tsin if necessary.
7 Dilute remaining cornflour in cold water, stir into the pan, cook for 1 minute until the sauce thickens and acquires a characteristic translucency, and serve.

Duck with almonds

cooking time   30—45 minutes

you will need for 6 servings:

3 tablespoons oil	2 tablespoons celery,
1 teaspoon salt	diced
1 lb. raw duck, diced	2 oz. mushrooms, sliced
2 tablespoons soya sauce	½ pint boiling water
8 oz. peas	1 tablespoon cornflour
	4 oz. roasted almonds

1 Heat oil with salt, add duck and cook gently until nearly done (the time would vary, depending on the age of duck).
2 Add soya sauce, vegetables and water.
3 Stir, bring to the boil, cover and simmer for 5—7 minutes.
4 Add cornflour, diluted with 3 tablespoons cold water, and cook, stirring until sauce thickens, add almonds, mix and serve.

Sweet and sour duck

cooking time   35—40 minutes

you will need for 6 servings:

1 duck, singed and	breadcrumbs
cleaned	oil for deep frying
salt	sweet sour sauce
1 egg, beaten	(see page 60)

1 Bone the duck but keep it whole.
2 Sprinkle with salt, brush well with egg, coat with breadcrumbs and repeat the operation to make breadcrumbs adhere.
3 Deep fry in oil until golden.
4 When cooked, drain, cut into uniform pieces and keep hot.
5 Prepare sweet sour sauce, pour over the duck and serve.

Duck with plum sauce

cooking time   7–8 minutes

you will need for 4 servings:

4–6 oz. breast of duck, uncooked	peanut oil for deep frying
2 cloves garlic, crushed	flour
pinch ginger	2 oz. (4 tablespoons)
pinch salt	plum sauce (canned)
pinch Ve-Tsin	pinch sugar
1 tablespoon Chinese wine (or sherry)	¼ pint chicken stock (or water with a bouillon cube)
1 egg, beaten	

1 Cut duck meat into thin slices, put in a shallow dish. Add garlic.
2 Sprinkle with ginger, salt, Ve-Tsin and wine. Mix well and leave to stand for 5 minutes. Then remove and throw away the garlic.
3 Add egg to pieces of duck and stir to coat all pieces well.
4 Heat oil for deep frying.
5 Dredge pieces of duck lightly with flour, deep fry until golden, drain and keep warm.
6 Heat plum sauce in a pan, add sugar and stock, bring to the boil, rub through a sieve and serve with deep fried duck.

Duck with salt lemon and ginger sauce

cooking time   1 hour

you will need for 6 servings:

1 salt lemon	1 duck, (about 3 lb.) cleaned and drawn
1 oz. fresh ginger	boiling water
½ pint vinegar	4 oz. Chinese pickled ginger
1 dessertspoon sugar	
1 teaspoon sesame oil	

1 Shred lemon skin finely, having first scraped off the pith.
2 Chop fresh ginger finely and mix with lemon skin, vinegar, sugar and sesame oil. Blend well.
3 Put the duck into a large pan of boiling water.
4 Bring to the boil, simmer for 45 minutes and allow to cool in the same water.
5 Bone the duck and cut the meat into very thin slices.
6 Slice the pickled ginger and line a dish with it. On this foundation put the duck slices.
7 Bring the lemon and ginger sauce to the boil, pour over the duck, and serve.

Fried duck with sweet sour sauce

cooking time   5 minutes

you will need for 4 servings:

6 oz. duck meat, sliced	1 oz. celery, sliced
1 oz. bamboo shoots, sliced	½ oz. Chinese pickled onions
2 oz. onions, sliced	¼ oz. lichen (Wun Yee)
1 oz. water chestnuts, sliced	sweet sour sauce (see page 60)
1 oz. fresh mushrooms, sliced	

1 Put all ingredients, except duck and sweet sour sauce, into a hot oiled pan and cook for 2 minutes.
2 Add duck and cook for 2 minutes.
3 Cover with sweet sour sauce, cook for 1 minute and serve.

Duck with prawns and bamboo shoots

cooking time   2 hours 15 minutes

you will need for 6 servings:

1 duck (2½–2 lb.)	1 tablespoon oil
1 teaspoon salt	1 clove garlic, crushed
1 dessertspoon soya sauce	8 oz. prawns, shelled
1 tablespoon brandy	8 oz. fresh mushrooms, sliced
1 teaspoon cinnamon	2 pints water
8 oz. giblets	1 teaspoon cornflour
2 oz. bamboo shoots	

1 Clean and wash duck and rub with salt.
2 Combine soya sauce, brandy and cinnamon and rub the duck with this mixture.
3 Slice the giblets and bamboo shoots.
4 Heat oil with garlic in a large pan, put in duck and giblets, fry until brown.
5 Add prawns, bamboo shoots, mushrooms and the rest of the mixture used for painting the duck.
6 Add water, simmer gently for 2 hours, then add cornflour diluted with 2 tablespoons water.
7 Reheat and serve.

Roast duck (1)

cooking time   1 hour

you will need for 6 servings:

1 duck, singed and cleaned	3 cloves garlic, crushed
salt	1 oz. spring onions, chopped
2 tablespoons brandy	
1 dessertspoon soya sauce	

1 Rub duck with salt.
2 Mix 1 dessertspoon brandy, 1 teaspoon soya sauce, half the garlic and half the spring onions.
3 Stuff the duck with this mixture. (This is more in the nature of a seasoning than a stuffing.)
4 Sew up opening.
5 Mix the rest of the ingredients together and rub some of the mixture all over the duck.
6 Leave to stand until the mixture dries and repeat the rubbing process.
7 Roast the duck in the oven, using a grid in the pan for it to sit on.
8 Add a little water to the pan and brush the duck with the remainder of the mixture every 15 minutes.
9 Brown the bird well, reduce the pan juices and serve with the duck.

Roast duck (2)

cooking time 1 hour

you will need for 6 servings:

1 duck, singed and cleaned	¼ pint Chinese wine
2 tablespoons soya sauce	(or vermouth)
4–5 cloves garlic	salt to taste
2–3 slices green ginger	½ pint water
2 dessertspoons sugar	4 peeled pears cut
1 tablespoon peanut oil	into halves

1 Paint duck with some of the soya sauce.
2 Crush garlic and ginger and combine all the ingredients (except duck) and bring to the boil.
3 Sew up neck opening, pour contents of saucepan into tail opening of duck, and sew up.
4 Start roasting in a hot oven for first 10 minutes, then reduce heat and roast slowly for 45–50 minutes.
5 Remove, allow to get cold, then cut into uniform small slices.
6 Arrange on a serving dish, and serve with the pan juices, strained and reheated, poured over it.
7 Garnish with pear halves.

Variations

Roast turkey

Proceed as in Roast duck, substituting a small turkey for the duck and allowing more cooking time, depending on size of bird, allowing 15 minutes per pound.

Roast turkey stuffed with braised noodles

Stuff the turkey with braised noodles, prepared as described on page 79, and roast as above.

Braised pigeons with sprouts

cooking time 12 minutes

you will need for 4–6 servings:

2 pigeons, singed and cleaned	2 slices green ginger
1 lb. sprouts	1 teaspoon sugar
2 tablespoons peanut oil	1 dessertspoon brandy
1 teaspoon salt	1 dessertspoon soya sauce
½ pint water	1 dessertspoon cornflour

1 Cut pigeons into small slices and prepare sprouts for cooking.
2 Heat half the oil in a pan, add ½ teaspoon salt and toss the sprouts in it for a few seconds, stirring constantly.
3 Add ¼ pint water and simmer for 3 minutes.
4 Take out sprouts and put aside.
5 In another pan, using the rest of the oil, fry the pigeons briskly with salt and ginger for ½ minute, stirring constantly.
6 Add sugar, brandy, soya sauce and water.
7 Simmer for 7–8 minutes.
8 Add sprouts with their pan juices. Cook for 1 minute.

9 Thicken the gravy with cornflour diluted with 2 tablespoons water, and serve.

Variations

Braised pigeon with cabbage

Proceed as in previous recipe, substituting 1 small diced cabbage for sprouts.

Braised pigeon with broccoli

Proceed as above, substituting 1 lb. broccoli, cut into small chunks, for cabbage.

Braised pigeon with cauliflower

Proceed as above, substituting 1 small cauliflower, divided into flowerets, for broccoli.

Braised pigeon with courgettes

Proceed as above, substituting 12 oz. sliced courgettes.

Braised pigeon with asparagus

Proceed as above, substituting 1 lb. asparagus for courgettes.

Braised pigeon with bamboo shoots and water chestnuts

Proceed as above, substituting 8 oz. sliced bamboo shoots and ½ dozen water chestnuts for asparagus.

Braised pigeon

cooking time 25–30 minutes

you will need for 4–6 servings:

2 pigeons, singed and washed	1 oz. preserved Chinese ginger, sliced
2 tablespoons soya sauce	and chopped
¼ pint water	salt and pepper
5–6 spring onions	

1 Braise pigeons whole with soya sauce and water for 25–30 minutes, turning frequently.
2 Leave to get cold, then slice and serve with spring onions and ginger.
3 Serve a small saucer of mixed salt and freshly ground pepper.

Fried spiced pigeons

cooking time 10 minutes

you will need for 4 servings:

2 pigeons, singed and cleaned	1 dessertspoon gin
½ teaspoon salt	pepper
½ teaspoon Chinese spice (Ng Heung Fun)	oil for deep frying

1 Cut each pigeon in half.
2 Put in bowl and sprinkle with salt, Chinese spice, gin and a little pepper.
3 Leave to macerate for 8 hours.
4 Deep fry the pigeons in oil until they turn golden.
5 Drain, sprinkle with spices in which they were macerated, and serve.

45

Fried pigeon

cooking time   15 minutes

you will need for 4–6 servings:

2 pigeons, singed and washed
oil
1 dessertspoon soya sauce
1 dessertspoon gin
1 teaspoon ginger root juice
sugar

1 Cut pigeons in half and sauté for 10 minutes in a pan with heated oil.
2 Combine soya sauce, gin, ginger root juice and sugar.
3 Add to pigeons, cover, simmer for 5 minutes and serve.

Fried pigeon with mixed vegetables

cooking time   4 minutes

Using 1 large or 2 small pigeons, proceed as described in the recipe for Fried chicken with mixed vegetables (see page 34), substituting pigeons for chicken.

Fried snipe with ginger juice

cooking time   6–7 minutes

you will need for 4 servings:

4 snipe
1 tablespoon light soya sauce
2 teaspoons sugar
1 tablespoon Chinese wine (or sherry)
1 tablespoon fresh ginger juice
oil for deep frying

1 Wash the birds and dry on a cloth.
2 Mix soya sauce, sugar, wine and ginger juice, paint the snipe with the mixture and leave to absorb the dressing for 30 minutes.
3 Heat oil and deep fry snipe until golden brown.

Fivespice pigeons

cooking time   35–40 minutes

you will need for 4–6 servings:

4 pigeons, drawn and cleaned
1 pint soya sauce
6 oz. sugar
1 tablespoon powdered cinnamon
2 aniseeds
1 pint water
oil for deep frying
3–4 spring onions, chopped
celery salt

1 Wash and dry the pigeons on a cloth.
2 Mix the soya sauce, sugar, cinnamon, aniseed and water in a deep, narrow pan.
3 Bring to the boil, add pigeons, reduce heat and simmer gently for 30 minutes.
4 Remove pigeons, wipe dry and deep fry in oil until brown.
5 Drain, cut into convenient pieces, sprinkle with spring onions and serve.
6 Serve celery salt in individual salt cellars, into which each person can dip the pieces of pigeon.

Quails in almond orchard

cooking time   25 minutes

you will need for 6 servings:

8 oz. bamboo shoots
water
4 oz. water chestnuts
2–3 quail, boned
8 oz. lean pork
1 tablespoon lard
1 tablespoon light coloured soya sauce
1 teaspoon salt
1 teaspoon Ve-Tsin
1 teaspoon cornflour
2 oz. almonds, slivered

1 Boil bamboo shoots in water for 15 minutes and drain. Then chop them with water chestnuts.
2 Mince the quail meat with the pork.
3 Heat lard and fry bamboo shoots and water chestnuts for 1 minute.
4 Add quail and pork mixture. Season with soya sauce, salt and Ve-Tsin. Cook for 5 minutes, stirring constantly.
5 Sprinkle with cornflour. Mix well, cook for a further 3–4 minutes. Remove to a heated serving dish, cover with almonds and serve.

Fish

The seas and rivers of China provide the country with an enormous variety of fish, and the Chinese certainly treat it with the gastronomic respect it deserves. There are many exotic and interesting ways of treating fish, and the recipes which follow include both the most popular Chinese fish dishes and those which help to present 'the same old plaice' in an exciting new way.

Whole bream with tomatoes

cooking time   6–7 minutes

you will need for 4–6 servings:

1 bream (1–1½ lb.), cleaned	1 teaspoon sugar
salt	1 teaspoon sherry
flour	1 teaspoon cornflour
4 tablespoons oil	¼ pint water
1 clove garlic, crushed	½ oz. spring onions
8 oz. ripe tomatoes, skinned and quartered	

1 Make a few light incisions, slantwise, on both sides of fish, taking care not to cut too deep.
2 Sprinkle with salt and dredge with flour.
3 Heat oil in a pan and cook fish gently until brown (4–5 minutes).
4 Remove and keep hot.
5 Pour off excess oil from pan, add garlic and tomatoes.
6 Blend sugar, sherry and cornflour with the water and add to the pan.
7 Simmer for 2 minutes.
8 Meanwhile cut the spring onions into 2-inch strips, then with a sharp knife slice them lengthwise.
9 Pour the sauce over the fish, sprinkle with spring onions and serve.

Fried fish with mushrooms

cooking time   6 minutes

you will need for 4 servings:

1 lb. fish (any round fish)	2 onions
1 tablespoon cornflour	1 oz. bamboo shoots
1 tablespoon cold water	2 oz. oil
2 oz. mushrooms	

1 Cut fish into thin slices.
2 Mix cornflour with water and dip fish in it.
3 Slice mushrooms, onions and bamboo shoots and fry in a little oil for 3 minutes.
4 Remove vegetables, add rest of oil, heat and fry the fish for 2 minutes, turning carefully.
5 Put back the onions, mushrooms and bamboo shoots, add a tablespoon water, cover with lid and simmer for 1 minute.
(The dish is ready as soon as the fish turns white.)

Fish balls

cooking time   5 minutes

you will need for 4 servings:

1 lb. fish, boned and chopped	a little fish stock
salt and pepper	1 tablespoon vinegar
1 egg	1 dessertspoon oil
4 oz. cornflour	4–5 spring onions
	2 cloves garlic

1 Season the chopped fish with salt and pepper, add egg and cornflour.
2 Stir until the mixture is smooth and shape into small balls.
3 Use fish trimmings and bones to make a little stock.
4 Add to the stock, vinegar and a little oil.
5 Strain, reheat, and when it comes to the boil drop in the fish balls.
6 Simmer for 5 minutes.

Variation

Fish balls with sweet and sour sauce
Proceed as above, but instead of boiling the fish balls, deep fry them in oil until golden and serve with sweet and sour sauce (see page 60).

Fish balls in savoury sauce

cooking time   7–8 minutes

you will need for 4 servings:

2 tablespoons oil	2 tablespoons spring onions, minced
½ teaspoon salt	
¼ teaspoon pepper	2 tablespoons fish stock
2 tablespoons soya sauce	fish balls (see preceding recipe)

1 Heat oil with salt and pepper.
2 Add soya sauce, spring onions and fish stock.
3 Cook for 2 minutes, toss fish balls in mixture and serve.

Whole fish in 'hot and sour' soup

cooking time   25 minutes

you will need for 6 servings:

6 dried Chinese mushrooms	¼ pint vinegar
	1 onion, sliced
1 fish (3–3½ lb.) (mullet, bream, sea-trout)	2 cloves garlic
	2–3 dried chillis
2½ pints water	1 tablespoon soya sauce
salt	
6 peppercorns	

1 Soak the mushrooms in enough lukewarm water to cover for 20 minutes.
2 Drain and remove stalks.
3 Scale and wash the fish, but leave head and tail on. Put it in a pan or fish kettle, with water, salt, peppercorns, vinegar and onion.
4 Bring to the boil, skim, reduce heat and simmer for 15 minutes.
5 Crush garlic with chillis, dilute with soya sauce, blend well and add to fish soup.
6 Add mushroom caps, simmer 5 minutes.

Note:

Take care not to overcook or break the fish. Place it whole on a heated serving dish. Serve soups at the same time in separate bowls.

Sweet and sour fish

cooking time   7–8 minutes

you will need for 4–6 servings:

1 bream (1–1½ lb.) (or perch)	4 tablespoons oil
salt	sweet and sour sauce (see page 60)
flour	

1 Make a few shallow incisions, slantwise, on both sides of the fish, 3–4 cuts on each side, depending on size.
2 Season with salt and coat with plain flour, making sure that the flour adheres properly.
3 Heat the oil and fry the fish whole until brown.
4 Place on a serving dish and cover with sweet and sour sauce.

Sweet and sour fillets of fish

cooking time   5 minutes

you will need for 4 servings:

8 oz. cod, filleted	1 tablespoon oil
1 egg, beaten	sweet and sour sauce
cornflour	(see page 60)

1 Slice the fillets thinly and dip in egg and cornflour.
2 Heat oil in pan and fry fish, turning carefully, for 3 minutes. (When fish turns white it is ready.)
3 Add sauce. Stir, simmer for 2 minutes and serve.

Variation

Sweet and sour plaice
As above, allowing 4 plaice fillets, cut in strips, instead of cod.

Sweet and sour fish cakes

cooking time   5–6 minutes

you will need for 4 servings:

8 oz. cod, filleted (or other similar fish)	2 oz. cabbage, finely shredded
1 teaspoon salt	oil for frying
½ pint water	sweet and sour sauce
2 teaspoons soya sauce	(see page 60)
2–3 spring onions, chopped	

1 Flake the fish, then chop finely and put in a bowl.
2 Dilute salt in water, and little by little whisk this solution into the fish.
3 Add soya sauce, spring onions and cabbage.
4 Mix well, shape into fish cakes.
5 Fry in very hot oil until golden on both sides.
6 Serve with sweet and sour sauce.

Braised eel

cooking time   17–18 minutes

you will need for 4 servings:

1 lb. eels	1 small leek
1 oz. oil	3 cloves garlic, crushed
1 teaspoon sherry	1 teaspoon cornflour
2 tablespoons soya sauce	2 tablespoons cold water
½ pint stock	1 dessertspoon vinegar

1 Cut eels into 2-inch chunks.
2 Fry in oil for 5 minutes until brown all over.
3 Add sherry, soya sauce and stock.
4 Chop the leek, add to pan with the garlic. Cover and simmer for 12 minutes.
5 Dilute cornflour with water, add to the pan.
6 Bring to the boil, sprinkle in vinegar and serve.

Fried bream with black beans

cooking time   8–10 minutes

you will need for 4–6 servings:

1 bream (1–1½ lb.)	4 tablespoons oil
salt	1 dessertspoon cornflour
plain flour	½ pint water
1 oz. black soya beans	4–5 spring onions
1 teaspoon brandy	½ oz. cooked lean pork
1 clove garlic, crushed	1 teaspoon soya sauce

1 Make a few shallow incisions, slantwise, on both sides of fish.
2 Sprinkle with salt and coat with flour, making it adhere properly.
3 Scald the soya beans and mix with brandy and garlic.
4 Heat the oil in a large pan and fry the fish until golden.
5 Put on large serving dish and keep hot.
6 Pour off surplus oil from pan, fry the black bean mixture for 2 minutes, stirring constantly.
7 Blend cornflour with water, add to the pan, cooking for 2 minutes, stirring all the time.
8 Cut spring onions into 2-inch strips, then with a sharp knife into as many strips lengthwise as possible.
9 Add to the pan.
10 Shred the pork, place in the sauce to heat it. Pour over fish, sprinkle with soya sauce and serve.

Variation

Steamed bream with black beans

cooking time   15 minutes

Proceed as in previous recipe, but instead of cooking the black bean mixture separately, put it on top of the fish and steam. Garnish with spring onions and lean pork, shredded, and serve.

Steamed turbot (1)

cooking time   15 minutes

you will need for 4 servings:

4 oz. mushrooms, sliced	1 oz. oil (or other cooking
1 oz. onion, sliced	fat)
1 tablespoon soya sauce	1 teaspoon vinegar
1 lb. turbot	salt and pepper

1 Combine mushrooms and onions and season with soya sauce.
2 Wash fish, put in a deep dish.
3 Cover with mushrooms and onions, put in a steamer, sprinkle with oil and steam for 15 minutes with a lid on.
4 Season with vinegar, salt and pepper and serve.

Variation

Steamed sole or plaice
As above, with either fish, but cooking for 10 minutes only. When using sole, take care to put the fish into the dish white side up.

Mullet Shanghai style

cooking time   5 minutes

you will need for 4 servings:

1 mullet (2½–3 lb.)	2 tablespoons brown
3 spring onions, chopped	sugar
¼ pint (⅔ cup) soya sauce	2–3 tablespoons water
2–3 tablespoons sherry	lard for deep frying

1 Scale and wash mullet, remove head. Cut fish into steaks 1–inch thick, lay them in a bowl and sprinkle with spring onions.
2 Mix soya sauce with sherry, sugar and water, bring to the boil, allow to cool, pour over the slices of mullet and leave for 3 hours, turning them from time to time.
3 Heat lard. Drain mullet steaks, deep fry for 2½ minutes on each side, until crisp and golden. Drain and serve at once.

Note:

This recipe is equally successful when applied to bream.

Braised bream

cooking time   10 minutes

you will need for 4–6 servings:

1 bream (1–1½ lb.)	1 teaspoon soya sauce
salt	1 teaspoon sherry
flour	1 dessertspoon cornflour
4 oz. lean pork	1 pint water
few spring onions	1 clove garlic, crushed
4 tablespoons oil	2 teaspoons oyster sauce

1 Make a few shallow incisions slantwise each side of the fish, and sprinkle with salt.

2 Dredge with flour, coating it thoroughly.
3 Shred the pork and cut the spring onions into 2-inch strips and then shred them lengthwise.
4 Heat oil in pan large enough to take the fish, and fry the bream until it is golden brown.
5 Put on a dish and keep hot.
6 Pour off most of the oil from the pan, leaving just a film on the bottom.
7 Combine soya sauce, sherry and cornflour into a smooth paste and dilute with water.
8 Heat the pan, add garlic, sprinkle with salt and fry the shredded pork briskly.
9 As soon as it browns add oyster sauce. Blend well. Cook for 1 minute and add the cornflour mixture.
10 Put fish back in the pan, simmer together for 3 minutes. Sprinkle with spring onions and serve.

Sea bass—Hong Kong style

cooking time   21 minutes

you will need for 4 servings:

1 fresh sea bass (2 lb.)	¼ teaspoon cinnamon
1½ teaspoons salt	3 spring onions, cut in
4 tablespoons soya sauce	2-inch pieces and slit
1 teaspoon lemon peel,	lengthwise
finely grated	2 tablespoons oil
1 teaspoon powdered	
ginger	

1 Put the fish (whole) into a fish-kettle of boiling water, bring to the boil, simmer for 1 minute.
2 Cover, turn off heat and leave to stand for 20 minutes.
3 Drain gently, put on a dish, sprinkle with salt, soya sauce, lemon peel, ginger, cinnamon, spring onions and oil and serve.

Bass with Chinese pickles

cooking time   15 minutes

you will need for 6 servings:

1 bass (2 lb.) ready for	3 tablespoons sugar
cooking	3 tablespoons vinegar
1–1½ pints boiling water	1 tablespoon Chinese
¼ can Chinese pickles	wine (or sherry)
1 tablespoon lard	1 tablespoon cornflour
1 shallot, finely chopped	

1 Put the bass in a steamer over boiling water and steam for 15 minutes.
2 While the fish is cooking, shred the pickles.
3 Heat lard and cook shallot for 1 minute.
4 Add pickles, sugar, vinegar, wine and cornflour. Cook for 2 minutes.
5 Arrange the bass on a heated serving dish. Spoon pickles and sauce over it and serve at once.

Cod or hake with green vegetables

cooking time 10–12 minutes

you will need:

1 oz. dried Chinese mushrooms	1 oz. spring onions
1 lb. cod (or hake)	½ oz. fresh ginger
1 egg white, lightly beaten	oil for deep frying
1 teaspoon salt	1 tablespoon sherry
3 teaspoons cornflour	3 tablespoons water
4 oz. spring greens	2 teaspoons soya sauce
	pinch Ve-Tsin

1 Soak mushrooms in warm water for 30 minutes, drain, remove stalks.
2 Cut fish into pieces. Mix with egg white, a pinch of salt and 1 teaspoon cornflour.
3 Cook spring greens in salted water for 2–3 minutes and drain.
4 Cut onions, ginger, mushrooms and spring greens into strips.
5 Heat oil, deep fry fish pieces for 5–6 minutes, drain.
6 Fry vegetables and mushrooms in 1–2 table-spoons oil for 1 minute.
7 Add fish. Sprinkle the sides of the pan with sherry.
8 Blend remaining cornflour with water, soya sauce and Ve-Tsin, pour over contents of frying pan, cook for 1–2 minutes until the sauce thickens and serve.

Bass with tomato sauce

cooking time 7–8 minutes

you will need for 6 servings:

1 bass (1–1½ lb.) filleted	2½ tablespoons tomato sauce
salt	1 teaspoon soya sauce
6 oz. cornflour	1 dessertspoon sherry
oil for cooking	¾ pint water
	2 spring onions, chopped

1 Skin the bass fillets, cut into large dice and sprinkle with salt.
2 Reserve 1 dessertspoon cornflour for the sauce and mix the remainder with the fish, coating the fish thoroughly.
3 Fry fish in deep oil until golden, then drain and keep hot.
4 Combine tomato sauce, soya sauce, sherry and cornflour with water.
5 Bring to the boil, add fish, simmer for 3 minutes to ensure that fish is impregnated with the sauce.
6 Sprinkle with spring onions and serve.

Variation

Hake or cod with tomato sauce

As above, substituting either fish for the bass.

Bass with ginger sauce

cooking time 7–8 minutes

you will need for 4–6 servings:

1 bass (1½–2 lb.)	1 teaspoon ginger, chopped
1 dessertspoon salt	
water	2 oz. spring onions, chopped
1 dessertspoon soya sauce	
1 teaspoon oil	

1 Boil the fish with salt in plenty of water, bringing water to the boil before putting in the fish.
2 As soon as boiling is re-established, reduce heat and cook for 6 minutes.
3 Drain fish carefully and arrange on a serving dish.
4 Combine soya sauce, oil and ginger together, pour over the dish, garnish with spring onions and serve.

Note:

For this dish, fresh ginger is preferable to ground ginger.

Fish in crab sauce

cooking time 8–9 minutes

you will need for 4 servings:

oil for deep frying	1 teaspoon Ve-Tsin
1 lb. fish, boned	2 teaspoons cornflour
2 teaspoons salt	meat of 1 crab (or small can crab meat)
1 egg white, lightly beaten	¼ pint milk

1 Put oil to heat.
2 Wash the fish, dry on a cloth and cut into uniform bite-size pieces.
3 Put fish in a bowl, add 1 teaspoon salt, egg-white, Ve-Tsin and 1 teaspoon cornflour, mix well to coat all pieces and deep fry for 5–6 minutes, until crisp and golden.
4 Drain, put on a heated serving dish and keep warm.
5 Heat 2 tablespoons oil in a small pan, add crab meat, cook for ½ minute, add milk and remaining salt and cornflour.
6 Simmer for 1–2 minutes, until the sauce thickens, pour over fish and serve.

Braised carp

cooking time 25–30 minutes

you will need for 4–6 servings:

1 carp (2 lb.), scaled and cleaned (or grey mullet or bass)	1 onion, sliced
	1 teaspoon cornflour
2 oz. oil	1 pint stock (or water)
2 tablespoons soya sauce	1 teaspoon sherry
pinch ground ginger	1 teaspoon vinegar
1 clove garlic, crushed	salt and pepper

1 Fry the fish in smoking hot oil for 2–3 minutes, basting it thoroughly as it fries.
2 Sprinkle with soya sauce and ginger, add garlic and onion, laying them on top of the fish.
3 Reduce heat and simmer for 5 minutes to allow the flavours of the garnish to permeate the fish.
4 Dissolve cornflour in stock, pour over the fish, simmer gently for 15–20 minutes.
5 Sprinkle with sherry and vinegar, season to taste with salt and freshly ground pepper and serve.

Variation

Braised rock salmon or braised bass
Proceed as in previous recipe, substituting other fish for carp.

Braised abalone

cooking time 7–8 minutes

you will need for 4 servings:

1 can abalone	1 dessertspoon cornflour
1 dessertspoon oil	water
1 clove garlic, crushed	soya sauce
1 dessertspoon oyster sauce	

1 Cut abalone into thin slices.
2 Heat the oil, brown the garlic in it, add abalone and oyster sauce and cook for 5 minutes, stirring frequently.
3 Mix cornflour with liquid from the abalone can and water to bring the quantity up to $\frac{3}{4}$ pint.
4 Add to the pan and stir until the sauce thickens.
5 Simmer for a few minutes, add soya sauce and serve.

Braised sliced abalone

cooking time 10 hours 2 minutes

you will need for 4 servings:

8 oz. dried abalone	$\frac{1}{2}$ teaspoon cornflour
water	pinch Ve-Tsin
1 teaspoon lard	1 tablespoon oyster sauce

1 Wash abalones, put in a saucepan, add enough water to cover, bring to the boil, simmer for 2 hours, adding more water when necessary to keep the abalone just covered.
2 Drain, put in a rinsed pan, cover with fresh water and cook for 8 hours, until the abalone is tender.

3 Drain, keep some of the liquid.
4 Slice the abalone, lightly fry in lard for $\frac{1}{2}$ minute.
5 Dilute cornflour with 3 tablespoons of the liquid in which the abalone was braised.
6 Add Ve-Tsin and oyster sauce, blend well and pour the mixture over the abalone.
7 Simmer, stirring, for $1\frac{1}{2}$ minutes and serve.

Abalone in oyster sauce

cooking time 7–8 minutes

you will need for 4 servings:

1 can abalone	pinch sugar
2 tablespoons peanut oil	1 teaspoon dark soya
1 tablespoon Chinese wine (or sherry)	sauce
2 tablespoons stock	1 teaspoon chestnut powder (or cornflour)
few drops sesame oil	1 tablespoon water
2 tablespoons oyster sauce	

1 Drain the abalone, keeping all the juices, and slice into pieces about 1-inch square and $\frac{1}{2}$-inch thick.
2 Heat oil, add wine, stock, sesame oil, oyster sauce, sugar and soya sauce. Bring to the boil, then simmer for 5 minutes.
3 Add abalone, cook, stirring constantly for 2 minutes.
4 Dilute chestnut powder with water and abalone juice, blend into the pan and serve at once.

Crispy bream

cooking time 5–6 minutes

you will need for 4–6 servings:

1 bream ($1\frac{1}{2}$–2 lb.)	8 tablespoons oil
salt	

1 Clean fish but do not fillet. Salt liberally inside and out.
2 Heat oil in pan but do not allow to smoke.
3 Spoon some of this hot fat over one side of the fish, holding the fish over the pan.
4 Fry until lower side is crisp, basting the upper side all the time.
5 Remove from heat and leave the pan to stand until it cools.
6 Carefully turn the fish over and cook until the second side is crisp.

Note:

This method of frying fish, allowing the oil to cool before turning it, makes the fish crisp. Fish fried in this way can be served plain as it is, or with sweet and sour sauce, see page 60.

Chinese fish kromeskis

cooking time   5–6 minutes

you will need for 6 servings:

1 halibut (1½ lb.), filleted	¼ pint water
4 oz. lean ham, sliced	salt and pepper
1 oz. spring onions	½ oz. assorted shelled nuts
1 teaspoon soya sauce	2 tablespoons oil
1 teaspoon brandy	1 dessertspoon oyster sauce
2 tablespoons cornflour	

1 Skin the fish, cut into uniform oblong strips about 3-inches by 1½-inches and about ½-inch thick.
2 Beat them slightly to flatten.
3 Cut ham into similarly shaped strips, 1½-inches long and ¼-inch wide.
4 Cut spring onions into strips 1½-inches long.
5 Mix soya sauce, brandy and 1 dessertspoon cornflour, with the water.
6 Lay the rest of the cornflour on a piece of greaseproof paper.
7 Lay the fish slices on a board, sprinkle with salt.
8 Place on each slice a strip of ham, a piece of spring onion, and some chopped nuts.
9 Roll up the fish slices and seal with cornflour.
10 Dip these little cigar-shaped rolls in cornflour (a cocktail stick can be used for securing the rolls and must be removed before serving).
11 Heat the oil and fry the halibut rolls for 3 minutes, turning them carefully.
12 Add oyster sauce, cook for 2 minutes, stirring carefully, or shaking the pan from time to time to avoid damaging the rolls.
13 Add soya sauce and brandy. Bring to the boil, season with pepper to taste, and serve.

Fish rolls

cooking time   8–10 minutes

you will need for 6 servings:

1–1½ lb. fish, skinned and boned (hake, cod, haddock)	2 oz. ham, diced
	fat for deep frying
1 egg	½ oz. ginger, fresh chopped
1 teaspoon salt	
2 tablespoons cornflour	½ oz. spring onions, chopped
1–2 oz. mushrooms, sliced	
1 small can asparagus tips, drained and cut in chunks	4 tablespoons asparagus water
	½ tablespoon soya sauce
	pinch Ve-Tsin

1 Cut fish into thick fingers and make a slit in each piece, without cutting right through, but just to make a 'pocket'.

2 Beat egg with salt and 1 tablespoon cornflour, add fish and coat all pieces.
3 Insert a sliver of mushroom, a piece of asparagus and a small piece of ham into each 'pocket'. Roll up the pieces of fish, secure with cocktail sticks.
4 Heat fat and deep fry the fish rolls 6–7 minutes, until crisp and golden.
5 Drain, extract cocktail sticks and arrange fish rolls on a heated serving dish. Keep warm.
6 Mix ginger with spring onions, toss in a little oil in a frying pan, add whatever remains of mushrooms, asparagus and ham, cook for 1 minute.
7 Mix remaining tablespoon of cornflour with asparagus water, soya sauce and Ve-Tsin, pour over mixture in the frying pan, cook for 1–2 minutes until the sauce thickens, pour over fish rolls and serve.

Chinese fried haddock

cooking time   5 minutes

you will need for 4 servings:

1 haddock (1 lb.)	1 slice green ginger
salt	4–5 spring onions, chopped
1 dessertspoon brandy	
1–2 oz. oil	1 tablespoon vinegar
2 cloves garlic	

1 Sprinkle fish with salt and brandy and leave for 8–12 hours.
2 Cut into collops and fry in very hot oil until golden.
3 Pound the garlic and the ginger into a paste, add spring onions, blend with vinegar, sprinkle over the fish and serve.

Variation

Chinese fried whiting
Proceed as in previous recipe, substituting 1 lb. whiting (large-size) for haddock.

Abalone with bamboo shoots

cooking time   5 minutes

you will need for 4 servings:

oil	1 teaspoon sherry
1 can abalone, diced	stock to cover
8 oz. bamboo shoots, diced	1 teaspoon cornflour
	2 tablespoons cold water
salt	few drops sesame oil

1 Heat a little oil in pan, toss in abalone and bamboo shoots, season with salt to taste and quickly fry for 2 minutes.
2 Add sherry and stock. Cook for 2 minutes.
3 Add cornflour, diluted with water and sesame oil.
4 Simmer for 1 minute and serve.

Fried plaice, Hong Kong style

cooking time   6 minutes

you will need for 4 servings:

oil	stock to cover
3 oz. onion, chopped	8 oz. plaice, filleted
1 oz. celery, diced	½ teaspoon pepper
2 oz. water chestnuts, sliced	1 tablespoon Chinese wine (or sherry)
3 oz. bamboo shoots, sliced	1 teaspoon cornflour
	2 tablespoons cold water
2 oz. cucumber, sliced	1 teaspoon soya sauce
1 oz. mushrooms, sliced	few drops sesame oil

1 Heat a little oil in a pan and quick fry the vegetables, allowing no more than 1 minute.
2 Add stock and simmer under a lid for 1 minute.
3 Meanwhile, cut the fish into thin slices.
4 Remove vegetables from pan and arrange on a dish.
5 Put fish in another hot, oiled pan, add a little pepper and sherry. Cook for 1 minute, turning carefully.
6 Add vegetables to the fish and cook for 2 minutes.
7 Pour in cornflour diluted with water.
8 Season with soya sauce, sprinkle with sesame oil, cook for 1 minute and serve.

Plaice fillets with mixed vegetables and roasted almonds

cooking time   12–15 minutes

you will need for 6 servings:

1 lb. plaice fillets	2 tablespoons soya sauce
2 tablespoons flour	1 teaspoon sugar
1 egg	1 teaspoon cornflour
salt and pepper	2 tablespoons stock
½ pint peanut oil	(or water)
4 oz. mushrooms, sliced	2 oz. roasted almonds,
6 spring onions, chopped	slivered
4 oz. beans, sliced	

1 Cut the plaice (or other filleted fish) into bite-size strips.
2 Mix flour and egg to make a light batter, season with salt and pepper.
3 Heat oil. Dip fish in batter and fry until golden. Remove and keep warm.

4 Fry mushrooms, for 3 minutes, add onions and beans. Cook together, stirring constantly, for 3 minutes.
5 Add soya sauce, sprinkle in sugar. Dilute cornflour in stock, and blend into the pan. Cook uncovered for 2 minutes.
6 Transfer to a heated serving dish, lay strips of fish on top of vegetables, sprinkle with almonds and serve.

Stewed turbot with mixed vegetables

cooking time   15 minutes

you will need for 6 servings:

1 turbot (1¼ lb.), filleted	½ oz. onions
	soya sauce
salt and pepper	1 teaspoon sugar
flour	stock to cover
oil	1 teaspoon cornflour
½ oz. lily petals	2 tablespoons cold water
½ oz. preserved parsnips	few drops sesame oil
½ oz. fresh ginger	
1 oz. mushrooms	
2 oz. pork (lean)	

1 Skin the fish, put in a dish, sprinkle with salt and pepper and dredge with flour.
2 Deep fry, in boiling oil, for about 3 minutes.
3 Slice finely the lily petals, preserved parsnips, ginger, mushrooms, pork and onions, and put all these ingredients into a pot or pan with a little salt and the soya sauce.
4 Quick fry for 1 minute.
5 Add fish, sugar and stock. Simmer for 10 minutes.
6 Add cornflour diluted with water and sesame oil. Cook for 1 minute and serve.

Variations

Stewed sole with mixed vegetables
As above, substituting sole for turbot.

Stewed plaice with mixed vegetables
As above, substituting plaice for sole.

Fried sprats

cooking time   15 minutes

you will need for 4 servings:

1 lb. cleaned sprats	½ pint oil
1 egg, beaten	1 dessertspoon soya sauce
flour	

1 Coat sprats with egg and flour.
2 Deep fry in oil, putting in 4–5 fish at a time.
3 When they turn golden, remove, drain and sprinkle with a few drops of soya sauce.

Whiting in savoury sauce

cooking time   4–5 minutes

you will need for 4 servings:

1 whiting (1½ lb.)	¼ teaspoon pepper
2 tablespoons fish stock	4 tablespoons soya sauce
2 tablespoons oil	2 tablespoons spring
½ teaspoon salt	onions, finely chopped

1 Clean the whiting. Cut off heads and tails and use with any other trimmings for fish stock.
2 Heat oil with salt and pepper.
3 Sauté the whiting for 2 minutes. Pour soya sauce over the fish, sprinkle with spring onions and add stock.
4 Simmer gently under a lid for 2 minutes and serve.

Variations

Sole in savoury sauce
As above, substituting 12 oz. filleted sole for the whiting.

Turbot in savoury sauce
As above, using 12 oz.–1 lb. filleted turbot instead of sole.

Smelts in savoury sauce
As above, substituting 12 smelts for the turbot and allowing 5–6 minutes to sauté the smelts.

Sole with mushrooms and bamboo shoots

cooking time   6–7 minutes

you will need for 4 servings:

oil for deep frying	1 tablespoon fresh ginger,
½ lb. sole fillets, cut	cut into shreds
in 1½-inch pieces	2 spring onions, coarsely
2 tablespoons Chinese	chopped
wine (or sherry)	2 oz. mushrooms, sliced
1½ tablespoons light	2 oz. bamboo shoots,
coloured soya sauce	sliced canned
salt and pepper	pinch Ve-Tsin
3 teaspoons cornflour	2 tablespoons stock
1 egg white, lightly	(or water)
beaten	

1 Put oil to heat for deep frying.
2 Put fish in a bowl, add 1 tablespoon wine, 1 tablespoon soya sauce, a pinch each of salt and pepper, 2 teaspoons cornflour and mix well.
3 Stir in egg white.
4 Deep fry the sole pieces until golden brown, drain, put on a heated serving dish and keep warm.
5 Heat 2 tablespoons oil in a frying pan, add ginger and spring onions, fry for 1 minute.
6 Add mushrooms and bamboo shoots, fry for 1 minute.
7 Blend remaining cornflour with 1 tablespoon wine, Ve-Tsin and stock or water. Pour into the pan, cook stirring for 1–2 minutes, pour over sole and serve.

Sole with mixed vegetables

cooking time   7–8 minutes

you will need for 4 servings:

2 oz. bamboo shoots,	stock to cover
diced	8 oz. sole, filleted
2 oz. cucumber, diced	flour
2 oz. mushrooms, diced	1 teaspoon cornflour
oil	2 tablespoons cold water
salt and pepper	1 teaspoon soya sauce
1 teaspoon sugar	few drops sesame oil

1 Toss bamboo shoots, cucumber and mushrooms quickly in a hot oiled pan, allowing no more than 1 minute.
2 Sprinkle with salt and pepper, add sugar and stock.
3 Simmer for 3 minutes, meanwhile season the fish with salt and pepper and dredge with flour.
4 Heat oil in a pan and deep fry the fish for 2 minutes.
5 Add fish to vegetables and cook for 1 minute.
6 Blend in cornflour, diluted with water, soya sauce and sesame oil.

Note:

This recipe is equally good for plaice and other flat fish.

Sole on a plate

cooking time   25 minutes

you will need for 6 servings:

water	2–3 spring onions, cut in
1 whole sole (1½ lb.)	2-inch stalks
½ teaspoon salt	6 slices ham (Chinese,
1 tablespoon light soya	if possible)
sauce	6 slices bamboo shoots
pinch Ve-Tsin	1 tablespoon lard
2 tablespoons Chinese	1 teaspoon cornflour
wine (or sherry)	2–3 tablespoons stock
6 thin slices fresh ginger	

1 Put water to boil in a steamer.
2 Dip the fish in hot water for an instant, clean out, dry and sprinkle with salt, half the soya sauce, Ve-Tsin and half the wine.
3 Line a plate with 3 slices of ginger and the spring onions and lay the fish on top. Cover the sole with ham and bamboo shoots, place remaining slices of ginger on top. Put in a steamer and steam for 20 minutes.
4 Transfer sole to a heated serving dish and keep warm.
5 Heat lard in a frying pan, add all the vegetables, etc. which were steamed with the fish, and the remaining soya sauce and wine, blend in cornflour diluted in stock, bring to the boil, simmer for 1 minute.
6 Pour over the sole and serve.

Sturgeon with mixed vegetables

cooking time   5 minutes

you will need for 6 servings:

1½ lb. sturgeon, filleted	2 oz. celery, chopped
3 tablespoons oil	2 oz. bean sprouts
1 teaspoon salt	½ pint fish stock (made
½ teaspoon pepper	from the bones and
3 oz. fresh mushrooms,	trimmings)
sliced	3 tablespoons soya sauce
2 oz. bamboo shoots,	1 tablespoon cornflour
sliced	4 tablespoons cold water

1 Cut the fillets slantwise into ¼-inch strips.
2 Heat oil with salt and pepper and quickly fry the fish for 1 minute, then remove and keep hot.
3 In the same pan quickly toss the vegetables, then add stock.
4 Bring to the boil, cover and simmer gently for 3 minutes.
5 Put in the fish and add soya sauce, mixed with cornflour and water.
6 Stir until the sauce thickens and serve immediately.

Steamed turbot (2)

cooking time   10 minutes

you will need for 4 servings:

½ oz. lily petals	1 teaspoon salt
½ oz. spring onions	½ teaspoon soya sauce
½ oz. fresh ginger	1 teaspoon cornflour
¼ oz. preserved parsnips	2 tablespoons cold water
1 oz. mushrooms	1 lb. turbot
2 oz. lean pork	1 teaspoon oil

1 Cut the lily petals, spring onions, ginger, preserved parsnips and mushrooms into thin slices, and the pork into little strips.
2 Mix them together, sprinkle with salt and soya sauce, and add the cornflour diluted with water.
3 Put the fish on a dish, heap the other ingredients on top of it.
4 Steam for 10 minutes, sprinkle a little hot oil on top of it and serve at once.

Boiled sole with sweet sour sauce

cooking time   25 minutes

you will need for 4–6 servings:

1 sole (1–1½ lb.)	½ oz. preserved white
water	cucumber, sliced
½ oz. Chinese pickled	1 teaspoon shredded
onions	lemon zest
½ oz. onions	sesame oil
½ oz. fresh ginger	parsley, chopped
sweet sour sauce	

1 Skin the fish, put into a large pan of boiling water, cover and simmer gently for 20–25 minutes.

2 Take the fish out carefully, drain and put on a large dish.
3 Slice the Chinese pickled onions, onions and ginger finely.
4 Heat the sweet sour sauce, prepared as described in the recipe Sweet and Sour Pork on page 23.
5 Add cucumber, onions, ginger, Chinese pickled onions and lemon zest and simmer for 2 minutes.
6 Add a few drops of sesame oil and pile all the vegetables, with the sauce on top of the fish.
7 Sprinkle with parsley and serve at once.

Note:

This recipe is equally suitable for plaice, cod, haddock, and hake.

Fried oysters

cooking time   20 minutes

you will need for 4–6 servings:

2–2½ dozen oysters	½ pint water
salt and pepper	oil for deep frying
1 egg	chopped spring onions
2 oz. flour	

1 Season oysters with salt and pepper to taste.
2 Combine egg, flour and water to make a batter.
3 Dip oysters into it and deep fry. (As soon as they float up and turn golden, they are ready.)
4 Sprinkle with spring onions and serve.

Note:

Alternatively, the spring onions can be added to the batter.

Fried minced oysters

cooking time   9 minutes

you will need for 4 servings:

4 oz. dried oysters	1 dessertspoon sherry
1 oz. mushrooms, diced	1 teaspoon soya sauce
4 oz. water chestnuts,	salt and pepper
diced	1 teaspoon cornflour
4 oz. bamboo shoots,	2 tablespoons cold water
diced	2–3 small lettuce hearts,
oil	finely shredded

1 Put the oysters in a bowl, cover with hot water and leave to soak for 8 hours.
2 Chop the oysters, add to them mushrooms, water chestnuts and bamboo shoots.
3 Heat some oil in a pan and cook the mixture for 5 minutes.
4 Add sherry, soya sauce, and salt and pepper to taste. Cook for 3 minutes.
5 Add cornflour diluted with water, and cook for a further minute.
6 Line a dish with lettuce and serve the oyster mixture on top.

Stewed oysters

cooking time   2 hours 10 minutes

you will need for 6 servings:

6 oz. dried oysters	1 tablespoon oil
2 oz. dried Chinese	stock
mushrooms	2 teaspoons cornflour
6 oz. roast pork, sliced	3 tablespoons cold water
6 oz. bamboo shoots,	1 teaspoon soya sauce
sliced	salt and pepper
1 clove garlic, crushed	

1 Soak the oysters, as above, for 2 hours, then rinse well.
2 Soak mushrooms for 30 minutes, remove stalks. (See note on page 7.)
3 Cut the pork slices and bamboo shoots into uniform 1-inch by $\frac{1}{2}$-inch pieces.
4 Fry the garlic in a hot oiled pan for 10 seconds, remove it, put in the mushrooms, cook for 5 minutes.
5 Add oysters, pork and bamboo shoots and cook together for 2 minutes.
6 Transfer into a saucepan, add enough stock to cover and simmer gently for 2 hours.
7 Dilute the cornflour with water and add to the pan.
8 Sprinkle in soya sauce, season with salt and pepper and serve.

Cuttlefish with mushrooms and celery

cooking time   9 minutes

you will need for 4–6 servings:

1 tablespoon oil	4 oz. mushrooms, sliced
1 clove garlic, crushed	1 dessertspoon soya
1 lb. cuttlefish (or canned	sauce
awabi) in large dice	1 teaspoon sherry
$\frac{1}{2}$ teaspoon salt	1 dessertspoon cornflour
1 large onion cut in rings	$\frac{1}{2}$ pint water
4 oz. celery, diced	$\frac{1}{2}$ oz. spring onions cut in
$\frac{1}{4}$ teaspoon pepper	$1\frac{1}{2}$-inch strips

1 Heat the oil with the garlic.
2 Add cuttlefish, season with salt and sauté for 5 minutes.
3 Add onion, celery, pepper, and mushrooms and fry for 3 minutes.
4 Blend soya sauce, sherry, cornflour and water.
5 Pour into the pan, bring to the boil, add spring onions and serve.

Cuttlefish tails

cooking time   3–4 minutes

you will need for 4 servings:

6 tablespoons oil	1 tablespoon sherry
$\frac{1}{2}$ garlic clove, crushed	2 tablespoons hot water
$1\frac{1}{2}$ teaspoons salt	1 teaspoon sugar
12 fresh cuttlefish tails	2–3 spring onions, finely
(or canned awabi)	chopped
3 tablespoons soya sauce	

1 Heat oil with garlic and salt.
2 Add cuttlefish tails and brown quickly on both sides (2 minutes).
3 Mix soya sauce, sherry, hot water, and sugar, pour this mixture over the fish, cover.
4 Bring to the boil, sprinkle with spring onions and serve.

Deep fried lobster

cooking time   10 minutes

you will need for 4 servings:

1 lb. lobster	1 tablespoon water
2 tablespoons cornflour	$\frac{1}{2}$ pint oil for deep frying
1 egg	salt and pepper

1 Remove lobster flesh from shell and cut the meat into small pieces.
2 Mix cornflour, egg and water to make Chinese batter.
3 Bring oil to the boil.
4 Dip lobster into batter and drop the pieces one by one into smoking hot oil.
5 Fry gently until golden.
6 Drain, sprinkle with salt and pepper and serve.

Lobster with tomatoes

cooking time   10 minutes

you will need for 4–6 servings:

$\frac{1}{2}$ oz. corn noodles	1 oz. mushrooms, diced
oil	salt
8 oz. lobster meat,	8 oz. tomatoes, peeled
sliced	1 teaspoon cornflour
$\frac{1}{2}$ oz. bamboo shoots,	2 tablespoons cold water
sliced	few drops sesame oil
4 oz. bean sprouts	1 teaspoon sugar
3 oz. onions, sliced	1 teaspoon soya sauce
$\frac{1}{2}$ oz. celery, sliced	1 egg, beaten

1 Cook corn noodles in pan of boiling oil for 3 minutes and drain.
2 Heat 1 tablespoon oil in another pan and cook lobster for 1 minute.
3 Add to it bamboo shoots, bean sprouts, onions, celery and mushrooms. Salt to taste. Cook for 1 minute.
4 Add tomatoes and cook for 2 minutes.
5 Add cornflour diluted with water, sesame oil, sugar, soya sauce and corn noodles, and cook for 1 minute.

6 Put on a dish.

7 Put egg in hot oiled pan and cook for 2 minutes.

8 Place the resulting omelette over the lobster dish and serve.

Lobster with pork

cooking time   16–17 minutes

you will need for 4 servings:

2 live lobsters (about 1 lb. each)	1 teaspoon salt
4 tablespoons oil	½ teaspoon pepper
1 clove garlic, crushed	¾ pint boiling water
8 oz. pork, finely minced	1 teaspoon cornflour
3 tablespoons soya sauce	3 tablespoons cold water
1 teaspoon sugar	1 egg
	3–4 spring onions, chopped

1 Clean the lobsters as described in the recipe for Steamed lobster, Hong Kong style (see page 58), and cut into 1-inch pieces, shell and all.

2 Heat the oil with the garlic.

3 Add pork and fry briskly until brown.

4 Add soya sauce, stir; add sugar, salt, pepper, and boiling water. Blend well.

5 Add lobster pieces and cracked claws. Cook under a lid for 12 minutes.

6 Mix cornflour with water, add to the pan and stir until the sauce thickens and becomes smooth.

7 Turn off heat.

8 Whisk the egg lightly, pour over lobster, stir, add spring onions, stir again and serve.

Fried lobster with rice noodles

cooking time   5 minutes

you will need for 4 servings:

6 oz. thick rice noodles	2 oz. water chestnuts, sliced
hot water	
1 tablespoon oil	2 oz. bamboo shoots, sliced
8 oz. lobster meat, diced	
3 oz. bean sprouts	1 oz. celery, sliced
1 oz. mushrooms, sliced	salt
2 oz. cucumber, sliced	1 teaspoon sugar
	1 dessertspoon soya sauce
	stock to cover

1 Put the noodles in a bowl, cover with hot water and leave to stand for 30 minutes.

2 Heat oil in pan and sauté the lobster for 1 minute.

3 Add all the vegetables and cook together for 1 minute.

4 Add salt, sugar, soya sauce and stock.

5 Cook for 1 minute, add drained noodles, cook for 2 minutes and serve.

Fried lobster tails

cooking time   10 minutes

you will need for 4 servings:

1 medium-sized lobster	8 oz. toasted bread- crumbs
salt	
1 egg, beaten	oil for deep frying

1 Slice the shelled lobster tail into thick collops.

2 Season with salt, dip in egg and breadcrumbs.

3 Deep fry in smoking hot oil, a few collops at a time.

4 Drain on greaseproof paper and serve.

Ginger lobster

cooking time   9–10 minutes

you will need for 4 servings:

1 tablespoon cornflour	8 oz. lobster meat, diced
2 tablespoons cold water	1 teaspoon fresh ginger, minced
4 oz. mushrooms, sliced	
4 oz. lettuce hearts, shredded	4–5 spring onions, chopped
1 oz. oil	

1 Mix cornflour with water.

2 Fry mushrooms and lettuce, using half the oil, for 3 minutes. Remove.

3 Add rest of oil. Dip lobster into cornflour mixed with water and fry for 3 minutes.

4 Add fried vegetables and cook together for 3 minutes.

5 Add ginger and spring onions, blend in, and serve.

Fried lobster with bean sprouts

cooking time   4 minutes

you will need for 6 servings:

1 tablespoon oil	1 teaspoon sugar
8 oz. lobster meat, sliced	1 teaspoon cornflour
salt and pepper	2 tablespoons cold water
1½ lb. bean sprouts	½ oz. spring onions
stock	1 teaspoon sesame oil

1 Heat oil in pan, put in the lobster, cook for 1 minute, and season with salt to taste.

2 Add bean sprouts, toss together for 2 seconds, cover with stock and simmer for 1 minute.

3 Add pepper, sugar, and cornflour diluted with water and cook for 1 minute.

4 Cut the spring onions into 2-inch pieces and add to the pan.

5 Sprinkle in sesame oil. Cook for 1 minute, and serve.

Fried lobster with vegetables

cooking time   5 minutes

you will need for 6 servings:

1 tablespoon oil	stock to cover
6 oz. onions, sliced	1 lb. lobster meat, sliced
2 oz. celery, sliced	$\frac{1}{2}$ teaspoon pepper
4 oz. water chestnuts, sliced	1 dessertspoon sherry
6 oz. bamboo shoots, sliced	1 teaspoon cornflour
4 oz. cucumber, sliced	2 tablespoons cold water
2 oz. mushrooms, diced	few drops sesame oil
	1 teaspoon soya sauce

1 Heat half the oil in pan, add all vegetables and toss for 1 minute.
2 Add stock. Cover pan, and simmer for 1 minute.
3 Remove vegetables and put on a dish.
4 In another pan heat rest of the oil. Put in lobster slices.
5 Season with pepper, add sherry, and cook for 1 minute, stirring gently.
6 Add vegetables, cook together for 2 minutes.
7 Blend in cornflour diluted with water and sesame oil.
8 Sprinkle in soya sauce, cook for a further minute, and serve.

Braised lobster with cabbage

cooking time   5–6 minutes

you will need for 6 servings:

1 lb. lobster meat	$\frac{1}{2}$ pint water
1 bunch Chinese white cabbage (or savoy cabbage)	1 dessertspoon soya sauce
	1 teaspoon sugar
2 tablespoons oil	1 teaspoon brandy
1 teaspoon salt	1 dessertspoon cornflour
	2 tablespoons cold water

1 Cut lobster meat into fairly large dice and shred the cabbage.
2 Heat half the oil, sprinkle in $\frac{1}{2}$ teaspoon salt and quickly toss the cabbage in it, 'scrambling' for 8–10 seconds.
3 Add half the water, simmer for 2 minutes, remove from pan and keep warm.
4 Heat the rest of the oil, add salt and similarly quickly toss the lobster meat.
5 Add soya sauce, sugar, rest of the water, and the brandy.
6 Set alight. Stir. Simmer gently for 3 minutes, add cabbage.
7 Cook for a minute or so to reheat it, add cornflour mixed with water, blend and serve.

Variations

Braised lobster with courgettes
As above, substituting courgettes for cabbage.
Braised lobster with Brussels sprouts
As above, substituting Brussels sprouts for courgettes.

Braised lobster with cauliflower
As above, substituting cauliflower for Brussels sprouts.
Braised lobster with peas
As previous recipe, substituting 8 oz. fresh garden peas (or small packet frozen peas) for the cauliflower.
Braised lobster with string beans
As above, substituting beans for peas.
Braised lobster with asparagus tips
As above, substituting asparagus tips for beans.
Braised lobster with pimentos
As above, substituting pimentos for asparagus tips.
Braised lobster with bamboo shoots and water chestnuts
As above, substituting bamboo shoots, sliced, and water chestnuts for pimentos, and adding a couple of slices green ginger, shredded, to the lobster.

Lobster omelette

cooking time $4\frac{1}{2}$–5 minutes

you will need for 6 servings:

1 tablespoon oil	salt
1 oz. onions, chopped	6 eggs, beaten
6 oz. lobster meat, diced	pepper

1 Heat the oil, put in the onions and cook for 30 seconds.
2 Add lobster, cook for 2 minutes, season with salt to taste.
3 Pour on eggs, mix all together quickly, cook for 1 minute, sprinkle in pepper.
4 Shake the omelette gently to ensure even cooking.
5 Cook for 1 minute and serve.

Steamed lobster, Hong Kong style

cooking time   30 minutes

you will need for 4 servings:

4 small live lobsters	3 tablespoons spring onions, chopped
3 eggs	2 tablespoons oil
1 teaspoon salt	2 tablespoons soya sauce
$\frac{1}{2}$ teaspoon pepper	1 tablespoon brandy
1 teaspoon sugar	
4 oz. pork, finely minced	

1 Wash the lobsters, cut off heads, remove and crack claws, clean out and throw away digestive tracts.
2 Without taking flesh out of the shell, cut the lobsters in half lengthways, then across into 1-inch pieces.
3 Put them in a shallow heatproof dish.

4 Beat the eggs lightly, add all the other ingredients and seasoning, blend well.

5 Spread this mixture over the lobsters.

6 Put the dish on a grid in a fish kettle, with water reaching within 1 inch of the dish. Cover.

7 Bring the water to the boil, simmer gently for 30 minutes, reduce heat, and serve at once.

Lobster with fresh noodles and vegetables

cooking time   3–4 minutes

you will need for 4 servings:

3 bundles fresh egg noodles	6 oz. bean sprouts
oil	2 oz. mushrooms, sliced
¼ teaspoon salt	4 oz. onions, sliced
8 oz. lobster meat, sliced	pepper
2 oz. bamboo shoots, sliced	1 teaspoon cornflour
	2 tablespoons cold water
	few drops sesame oil

1 Shake out noodles to separate them.

2 Immerse in a pan of boiling oil for a few seconds, pressing them gently to the sides of the pan to form a nest.

3 Remove and put on a dish.

4 Heat a tablespoon of oil in a pan, sprinkle in ¼ teaspoon of salt, put in the lobster and cook for 1 minute.

5 Add bamboo shoots, bean sprouts, mushrooms and onions.

6 Season with pepper to taste and cook for 1 minute.

7 Add cornflour, diluted with water and sesame oil.

8 Simmer for 1 minute, then place the contents on top of the noodles and serve.

Scallops with eggs

cooking time   4–5 minutes

you will need for 6 servings:

5 tablespoons oil	12 oz. scallops
1 teaspoon salt	1 tablespoon soya sauce
¼ teaspoon pepper	4 eggs
2 tablespoons onions, chopped	2–3 spring onions, chopped

1 Heat the oil with salt and pepper and cook the onions until they become transparent.

2 Add the scallops (whole, if they are small, cut in pieces, if large).

3 Stir and simmer uncovered for 2–3 minutes. Sprinkle with soya sauce.

4 Beat the eggs lightly, mix with spring onions, pour over the scallops.

5 Cook just long enough to set the eggs and serve.

Scallops with sweet peppers (pimentos)

cooking time   3 minutes

you will need for 6 servings:

6–8 scallops	2 sweet peppers, seeded, shredded
1 tablespoon peanut oil (or lard)	2–3 thin slices fresh ginger
1 small onion, finely chopped	pinch salt

1 Cut each scallop into 3–4 thin round slices.

2 Fry in hot oil for 1 minute, stirring all the time.

3 Add onion, peppers, ginger and salt.

4 Cook together for 2 minutes stirring constantly and serve.

Scallops with mushrooms

cooking time   4 minutes

you will need for 6 servings:

6 fresh scallops	2–3 thin slices fresh ginger
6 oz. fresh mushrooms	1 tablespoon soya sauce
1½ tablespoons lard	pinch salt
1 shallot, finely chopped	pinch sugar

1 Cut each scallop into 3–4 round slices.

2 Slice mushrooms.

3 Fry scallops in hot lard, stirring all the time for 1 minute.

4 Add mushrooms and shallot; cook stirring for 1 minute.

5 Add the remaining ingredients, cook stirring for 2 minutes. Serve.

Sweet and sour scallops with pineapple

cooking time   7–8 minutes

you will need for 6 servings:

1 dozen scallops	1 pint oil
cold water	2–3 tablespoons plain flour
1 teaspoon salt	2 eggs, beaten
1 teaspoon sugar	
2 teaspoons soya sauce	

1 Soak the scallops in water for an hour to swell them. Drain and wipe.

2 Sprinkle with salt, sugar, and the soya sauce, and leave to macerate, for 20 minutes.

3 Heat the oil and while it is heating, roll scallops lightly in flour, then dip into egg.

4 Drop them one by one into boiling oil. Deep fry until golden and drain on greaseproof paper.

5 While the scallops are frying, prepare the sauce.

6 Immerse scallops in sauce and serve.

Sweet and sour sauce

cooking time 7 minutes

you will need for 6 servings:

1 dessertspoon peanut oil	1 small can pineapple cubes, shredded
2 tablespoons water	1 dessertspoon cornflour
2 tablespoons vinegar	2 tablespoons cold water
1 dessertspoon sugar	
1 teaspoon salt	

1 Heat the peanut oil.
2 Add water, vinegar, sugar and salt.
3 Bring to the boil, add pineapple and cornflour diluted with water.
4 Remove from heat.

Variations

Sweet and sour oysters with pineapple
As above, substituting oysters for scallops.
Sweet and sour lobster with pineapple
As above, substituting 1 lb. lobster meat, cut in large dice, for the oysters.

Fried scallops with water chestnuts and bamboo shoots

cooking time 6 minutes

you will need for 6 servings:

2 tablespoons oil	1 oz. mushrooms, finely sliced
3 oz. water chestnuts, finely sliced	white stock to cover
3 oz. bamboo shoots, finely sliced	6 fresh scallops, finely sliced
3 oz. onions, finely sliced	pepper
1 stalk celery, finely sliced	1 dessertspoon sherry
2 oz. cucumbers, finely sliced	1 teaspoon cornflour
	2 tablespoons cold water
	1 teaspoon sesame oil
	1 dessertspoon soya sauce

1 Heat half the oil, toss the vegetables quickly for 1 minute.
2 Add stock and simmer gently for 1 minute.
3 Remove vegetables and put on a dish.
4 Heat the rest of the oil in a pan, add scallops, sprinkle with pepper and sherry and cook for 1 minute.
5 Add vegetables and cook together for 2 minutes.
6 Add cornflour, diluted with water, sesame oil and soya sauce.
7 Cook for 1 minute and serve.

Scallops with broccoli

cooking time 9–10 minutes

you will need for 4 servings:

8 oz. broccoli	1 teaspoon green ginger, finely minced
1 teaspoon cornflour	2 cloves garlic, crushed
¼ pint water	8 oz. scallops
1 dessertspoon soya sauce	salt and pepper
1 tablespoon oil	1 dessertspoon brandy

1 Cut broccoli into small chunks.
2 Mix cornflour with water and add soya sauce to it.
3 Heat oil in pan with ginger and garlic and fry the scallops for 4 minutes, seasoning them well with salt and pepper.
4 Add broccoli and cook for 3–4 minutes.
5 Pour in soya and cornflour mixture, bring to the boil.
6 Light the brandy and immediately pour into the pan. Blend and serve at once.

Note:

The same recipe can be made substituting any of the following vegetables for the broccoli: pimentos, asparagus tips, white cabbage or Brussels sprouts.

Crab au gratin à la Chinoise

cooking time 12–15 minutes

you will need for 4 servings:

1 cooked dressed crab	salt
4 oz. lean pork	1 egg
4 oz. fresh mushrooms	2 tablespoons bread-crumbs
4 or 5 spring onions, chopped	1 teaspoon sesame oil

1 Chop crab, pork, and mushrooms finely. Mix well.
2 Incorporate spring onions, season with salt, bind with egg, put back into the shell.
3 Sprinkle with breadcrumbs and sesame oil and cook in the oven or under the grill.

Crab with black beans

cooking time 45 minutes

you will need for 4 servings:

1 oz. black soya beans, scalded	1 dessertspoon brandy
1 clove garlic, pounded	1 dessertspoon oil
2 slices green ginger, pounded	1 large dressed crab

1 Mash the beans with a fork.
2 Combine with the rest of the ingredients, except the crab.
3 Arrange the crab in its shell, pile the bean mixture on top.
4 Place in a steamer and steam gently for 45 minutes.

Variation

Crab with mushrooms
As above, substituting fresh mushrooms for black beans, and allowing 4 oz. mushrooms. Dried mushrooms can be used but, in addition to being scalded, should be left to soak in water for 2–3 hours.

Deep fried crab

cooking time 7–8 minutes

you will need for 4 servings:

1 large crab, cooked
1 egg
2 tablespoons milk
salt

3–4 tablespoons bread-crumbs
oil for deep frying

1 Take the crab out of the shell and claws, without detaching any of the smaller legs.
2 Chop into 4 or more pieces depending on size, in such a way that each piece has a leg attached to it.
3 Beat egg with milk, add salt to taste, and holding each piece of crab by a leg, dip into egg and breadcrumbs.
4 Deep fry in very hot oil until golden.
5 Drain on greaseproof paper and serve.

Deep fried crab claws

cooking time 3–4 minutes

you will need for 4 servings:

4 crab claws, cooked
4–5 large prawns, cooked and shelled
salt and pepper

1 teaspoon Ve-Tsin
1 egg white, beaten
oil for deep frying
cornflour

1 Carefully extract the meat from the crab claws without breaking it.
2 Leave the tips of the shell on.
3 Pound the prawns, or put through a blender to reduce to a smooth purée. Season with salt and pepper to taste, add Ve-Tsin and fold in egg white to bind the forcemeat.
4 Using equal portions of the forcemeat, pack it around each claw, shaping it to the claw form.
5 Heat the oil.
6 Dust crab claws with cornflour, deep fry until golden and serve at once.

Crab kromeskis

cooking time 10–12 minutes

you will need for 4–6 servings:

1 lb. crab meat
2 oz. fresh mushrooms, chopped
1 oz. spring onions, chopped
1 tablespoon oyster sauce
salt and pepper
1 whole egg

1 egg, beaten
2 tablespoons cornflour
oil for deep frying
1 tablespoon brandy (or gin)
sweet sour sauce (see page 60)

1 Chop crab meat, combine with mushrooms, spring onions, oyster sauce, salt and pepper to taste, and bind with an egg.
2 Shape into little balls, dip in beaten egg and cornflour.
3 Heat the oil, add to it brandy or gin, and deep fry the kromeskis until golden.
4 Drain and serve with sweet sour sauce.

Crab Hong Kong style

cooking time 10 minutes

you will need for 6 servings:

2 large, soft shell crabs (or canned crab)
4 tablespoons oil for cooking
1 small clove garlic, crushed
4 oz. fresh pork, minced
1 teaspoon salt
2 tablespoons soya sauce

1 teaspoon sugar
½ teaspoon pepper
½ pint boiling water (or stock)
1 teaspoon cornflour
2 tablespoons cold water
1 egg, lightly beaten
2–3 spring onions, chopped

1 Clean and wash the crabs and cut into 6–8 pieces.
2 Heat the oil with the garlic, add pork, and salt, and brown lightly (2 minutes).
3 Pour in soya sauce, stir, add sugar, pepper, and stock.
4 Add crab pieces, mix well, cover, simmer for 7–8 minutes.
5 Mix cornflour with water, stir into the pan until the sauce is smooth.
6 Turn off heat. Stir egg into the mixture, sprinkle with spring onions and serve at once.

Stewed crab with mushrooms

cooking time 7 minutes

you will need for 4–6 servings:

1½–2 lb. cooked crab
1 dessertspoon oil
8 oz. button mushrooms
1 teaspoon soya sauce
1 teaspoon brandy

1 dessertspoon cornflour
3 tablespoons cold water
salt and pepper
1 knob green ginger, minced

1 Take the crab meat out of the shells and quick fry in oil for 2 minutes, stirring constantly.
2 Add mushrooms and cook together for 1 minute.
3 Add soya sauce, brandy and cornflour diluted with water.
4 Cook for 3 minutes.
5 Add salt and pepper to taste, sprinkle in green ginger, cook for 1 minute and serve.

Crab Foo Yung

cooking time   7–8 minutes

you will need for 4–6 servings:

4 oz. dried mushrooms
2 large soft shell crabs
  (or canned crab)
6 oz. onions, chopped
2 oz. water chestnuts,
  thinly sliced
2 oz. bean sprouts

5–6 eggs
2 teaspoons soya sauce
a little oil
1 tablespoon cornflour
$\frac{1}{4}$ pint stock (or water)
$\frac{1}{4}$ teaspoon sugar

1 Soak the mushrooms in warm water for 1 hour until soft, drain, remove stalks, then chop.
2 Shred the crab meat and blend thoroughly with onions, water chestnuts, bean sprouts, mushrooms, eggs, and 1 teaspoon soya sauce.
3 Heat a shallow pan with oil.
4 Take up a spoonful of the mixture at a time and drop into the oil.
5 Brown on both sides.
6 Mix the cornflour with soya sauce, stock, and sugar, and cook over low heat.
7 Pour over the Foo Yung and serve at once.

Crab omelette

cooking time   5 minutes

you will need for 4 servings:

3–4 eggs
generous $\frac{1}{4}$ pint milk
$\frac{1}{2}$ teaspoon Ve-Tsin
salt and pepper
a little oil
4 oz. crab meat

2 oz. mushrooms, sliced
1 oz. bamboo shoots,
  sliced
1 oz. spring onions,
  chopped

1 Beat eggs, add milk, Ve-Tsin, salt and pepper.
2 Heat oil in pan and quick fry the crab meat for 2 minutes.
3 Add mushrooms and bamboo shoots, cook together for 2 minutes.
4 Put spring onions into the egg mixture and pour into the pan.
5 Separately prepare the omelette sauce:

Sauce

cooking time   5 minutes

you will need for 4 servings:

1 dessertspoon oyster
  sauce
1 teaspoon soya sauce

1 teaspoon cornflour
2–3 tablespoons cold
  water

1 Combine oyster sauce, soya sauce and cornflour mixed with enough water to make a thin paste.
2 Bring to the boil.
3 Fold the pancake, put on a serving dish, pour the sauce over it, and serve.

Crab with eggs

cooking time   5 minutes

you will need for 4 servings:

1 small onion
2 tablespoons oil
1 teaspoon salt
$\frac{1}{2}$ teaspoon pepper

1 large dressed crab
6 eggs, beaten
2–3 spring onions, cut
  in 1-inch lengths

1 Slice the onion in very thin long strips and cook in oil until transparent.
2 Season with salt and pepper.
3 Add crab meat and fry quickly for 2–3 minutes, stirring all the time.
4 Pour in eggs, cook long enough for the eggs to set.
5 Sprinkle with spring onions and serve.

Prawns with chilli sauce

cooking time   9–10 minutes

you will need for 4–6 servings:

1 lb. uncooked Dublin
  Bay prawns
1 dessertspoon oil
$\frac{1}{2}$ clove garlic, chopped
$\frac{1}{2}$ teaspoon green ginger,
  chopped

1 tablespoon tomato
  sauce
1 teaspoon chilli sauce
$\frac{1}{4}$ pint water
4–5 spring onions,
  chopped

1 Do not shell the prawns but merely remove the heads.
2 Put oil in pan with garlic, and as soon as the oil gets hot add prawns and ginger.
3 Sauté briskly, shaking the pan all the time to prevent sticking.
4 As soon as prawns change colour, add tomato and chilli sauces.
5 Blend them in, add water, bring to the boil, simmer for 6 minutes.
6 Sprinkle with spring onions and serve.

Prawns with celery

cooking time   8 minutes

you will need for 4 servings:

1 dessertspoon oil
8 oz. cooked prawns,
  peeled
1 medium-sized onion,
  sliced
2 oz. mushrooms, chopped
3 oz. celery, sliced

pepper
1 teaspoon soya sauce
1 teaspoon brandy
1 teaspoon cornflour
$\frac{1}{4}$ pint water
4–5 spring onions, cut
  into 2-inch strips

1 Heat oil in pan and fry prawns and onion together for 3 minutes, stirring constantly.
2 Add mushrooms, celery, and pepper to taste.
3 Cook for 4 minutes.
4 Combine soya sauce, brandy, cornflour and water, and pour into the pan.
5 Cook for 1 minute. Serve, sprinkled with spring onions.

Prawns with pimentos

cooking time   8–9 minutes

you will need for 4 servings:

1 lb. shelled prawns, uncooked	1 knob green ginger, shredded
1 lb. pimentos	1 teaspoon sugar
2 tablespoons oil	1 dessertspoon soya sauce
1 teaspoon salt	2 oz. cucumber, sliced
5 tablespoons water	1 teaspoon sherry
	1 teaspoon cornflour

1 Split the prawns lengthwise and remove intestinal cord.
2 Cut pimentos, remove core and seeds and slice into half rings.
3 Heat 1 tablespoon oil in pan, add ½ teaspoon salt and quickly toss the pimentos for a few seconds.
4 Add 1 tablespoon water and simmer for 3 minutes.
5 Remove from pan and keep hot.
6 Heat the rest of the oil, add remainder salt and ginger, and sauté the prawns briskly for ½ minute.
7 Add sugar, soya sauce, cucumber, sherry, and 2 tablespoons water, simmer for 3 minutes, add pimentos and their juice. Mix.
8 Cook together for 1 minute, add cornflour diluted with 2 tablespoons water, and serve.

Variations

Prawns with courgettes
As above, substituting courgettes for pimentos.

Prawns with broccoli
As above, substituting broccoli for courgettes.

Prawns with cauliflower
As above, substituting cauliflower for broccoli.

Prawns with Brussels sprouts
As in previous recipe, substituting Brussels sprouts for cauliflower.

Prawns with asparagus tips
As above, substituting asparagus tips for Brussels sprouts.

Prawns with white cabbage
As above, substituting white cabbage for asparagus tips.

Prawns with bamboo shoots and water chestnuts
As above, substituting bamboo shoots, sliced and water chestnuts for white cabbage.

Prawns with mixed vegetables
As above, replacing bamboo shoots and water chestnuts by 4 oz. beans, 1 medium-sized onion, chopped, 2 medium-sized stalks celery, 4 oz. bean sprouts and 4 oz. tomatoes, peeled.

Prawns with cucumber

cooking time   5 minutes

you will need for 4 servings:

3 smallish cucumbers	3 tablespoons oil
1 lb. fresh prawns	2 tablespoons soya sauce
1 tablespoon cornflour (for dredging)	1 teaspoon sugar
½ teaspoon salt	½ teaspoon cornflour (for thickening)
1 tablespoon sherry	2 tablespoons cold water

1 Peel the cucumbers and cut into quarters lengthwise, then into 2-inch chunks.
2 Shell and clean prawns, dredge with a mixture of cornflour, salt, and sherry.
3 Heat pan, add 2 tablespoons oil, fry prawns for 3 minutes. Drain.
4 Add remaining tablespoon oil to pan, reheat and fry cucumber for a few seconds.
5 Add soya sauce, sugar, and cornflour mixed with water.
6 Blend well, simmer for 1 minute, add prawns, heat thoroughly and serve.

Prawn crackers (or Shrimp slices)

cooking time   4–6 minutes

you will need for 4 servings:

peanut oil, for deep frying	1 can prawn crackers

1 Heat the oil, drop into it a few cracker pellets at a time.
2 As soon as they open up and float up to the surface – this takes only a few seconds – take them out with a perforated spoon and drain.

Note:

They should become much larger in size but on no account should they be allowed to brown, therefore, care should be taken not to overheat the oil. If the crackers tend to turn even a pale brown, reduce heat.

Prawn fritters

cooking time   7–8 minutes

you will need for 4 servings:

1 egg	1 lb. prawns, shelled and minced
6 tablespoons flour	oil for deep frying
½ teaspoon salt	
½ pint milk	
1 oz. spring onions, chopped	

1 Make a batter incorporating the egg, flour, salt, milk, and spring onions.
2 Whisk well. Add prawns. Blend well to ensure smoothness of mixture.
3 Heat oil to boiling point and, taking a dessert-spoon at a time of the prawn mixture, deep fry the fritters until golden.
4 Drain and serve at once.

Prawn croquettes

cooking time   5–6 minutes

you will need for 4 servings:

1 lb. cooked prawns, peeled	2 raw egg yolks
salt and pepper	2 egg whites, stiffly beaten
½ tablespoon parsley, chopped	flour
1½ teaspoons soya sauce	peanut oil for deep frying

1 Mince or chop the prawns finely. Add salt, pepper, parsley, soya sauce and yolks. Mix well.
2 Fold in egg whites. Shape into small croquettes, roll in flour.
3 Deep fry for 5–6 minutes, until crisp and golden, drain on paper and serve at once.

Prawns with lettuce

cooking time   3 minutes

you will need for 4 servings:

1 lb. Dublin Bay prawns	1 tablespoon oil
salt and pepper	1 clove garlic, crushed
2–3 slices green ginger, pounded	1 lettuce, coarsely shredded
1 dessertspoon cornflour	¼ pint water

1 Peel prawns, leaving tail tips on.
2 Split prawns lengthwise and remove intestinal cord.
3 Sprinkle with salt and pepper, green ginger, and cornflour.
4 Heat oil in pan with garlic, add prawns and sauté briskly.
5 As soon as the prawns change colour add lettuce, cook for 1 minute.
6 Season to taste, add water, bring to the boil, stir and serve.

Prawn cutlets

cooking time   7–8 minutes

you will need for 4 servings:

1 lb. uncooked Dublin Bay prawns	4 oz. fresh breadcrumbs
salt	oil for deep frying
1 egg, beaten	2 tablespoons gin

1 Peel prawns leaving tail tips on.
2 Split prawns lengthwise, remove intestinal cord and flatten the cutlets slightly.
3 Sprinkle with salt.
4 Dip in egg and breadcrumbs, coating them thoroughly.
5 Bring oil to the boil with gin, and deep fry the prawn cutlets until light golden.
6 Drain and serve at once.

Prawn cutlets stuffed with almonds

cooking time   7–8 minutes

you will need for 4–6 servings:

1 lb. uncooked Dublin Bay prawns	salt
1–2 rashers lean bacon	1 egg, beaten
2 oz. almonds, blanched and roasted	flour
	oil

1 Peel the prawns and make a slit in them without opening them out.
2 Shred the bacon and chop the almonds, put ½ teaspoon of this mixture into each slit in the prawn.
3 Push edges of slit gently together.
4 Season with salt.
5 Dip in egg, dredge with flour and deep fry in smoking hot oil until golden.
6 Drain and serve at once.

Variation

Prawn cutlets stuffed with walnuts

As above, replacing almonds and bacon by shelled, skinned walnuts and lean ham.

Prawn balls

cooking time   7–8 minutes

you will need for 4 servings:

1 lb. fresh prawns	1 tablespoon sherry
10 water chestnuts, finely chopped	½ teaspoon salt
1 tablespoon cornflour	1 egg, lightly beaten
	oil for deep frying

1 Shell, wash, dry, and chop the prawns finely, or pass through a mincer.
2 Add water chestnuts and mix well.
3 Blend in cornflour, sherry, salt, and egg.
4 Form into balls, deep fry until golden and serve at once.

Prawn and pork cakes

cooking time   5 minutes

you will need for 6 servings:

¾ lb. prawns, peeled	1 teaspoon salt
6 oz. pork	small pinch sugar
1 tablespoon cornflour	3 tablespoons cold water
1 tablespoon Chinese wine (or sherry)	1–2 tablespoons oil (or lard)
1 tablespoon soya sauce	

1 Mince prawns and pork, put in a mixing bowl.
2 Sprinkle with cornflour, wine, soya sauce, salt, sugar and water.
3 Mix well.
4 Taking a dessertspoon of the mixture at a time, shape into cakes, as you would for fishcakes.

5 Heat oil and fry the cakes for 2½ minutes each side. Serve at once. Excellent with branch spinach.

Prawns with almonds
cooking time   9–10 minutes

you will need for 4–6 servings:

4 oz. almonds, blanched	1 clove garlic, crushed
salt	pepper
1 lb. large prawns,	2 oz. celery, finely
uncooked	chopped
1 slice ginger, pounded	1 teaspoon soya sauce
1 dessertspoon cornflour	1 teaspoon brandy
1 tablespoon oil	2 tablespoons water

1 Toss the almonds with salt in a slightly greased pan, just enough to turn them lightly golden.
2 Be careful not to burn.
3 Drain on greaseproof paper.
4 Peel the prawns, leaving the tail tips on.
5 Split the prawns lengthwise and remove intestinal cord.
6 Sprinkle with salt, put in a basin, add ginger, and cornflour and mix well.
7 Heat oil in pan, add garlic, cook for 1 minute, then remove garlic.
8 Put in the prawns and cook for 3 minutes, stirring constantly.
9 Season with pepper, add celery and cook for 3 more minutes.
10 Add soya sauce and brandy.
11 Rinse the basin in which the prawns were mixed with the water, and pour into the pan. Bring to the boil.
12 Add almonds, stir, allow to come to the boil once more, and serve.

Variation

Prawns with walnuts
As above, substituting shelled, skinned walnuts for almonds but omitting the roasting process for the nuts.

Prawn rolls
cooking time   20–25 minutes

you will need for 4–6 servings:

8 oz. fresh prawns,	½ teaspoon salt
shelled and chopped	1 teaspoon sugar
4 oz. water chestnuts,	½ teaspoon pepper
minced	few bacon rinds
4 oz. lean pork, minced	4 eggs, well-beaten
1 teaspoon sesame oil	oil for deep frying

1 Mix together prawns, water chestnuts, pork, sesame oil, salt, sugar, and pepper.

2 Chop together into a smooth mixture.
3 Heat a small frying pan with some bacon rinds to grease it.
4 Remove bacon rinds, and ladling out a little of the egg, just enough to cover bottom of pan, cook for 2 minutes on a low heat.
5 Turn out the pancake, flat, on a board.
6 Spread pancake evenly with prawn mixture, roll up, and turn in ends.
7 Continue until all egg and prawn stuffing is used up.
8 Put prawn rolls on a dish and steam for 10 minutes.
9 Heat the oil and then deep fry the rolls in it, allowing 4 minutes cooking time. Drain.
10 Cut rolls into 1-inch lengths and serve.

Variations

Lobster rolls
As above, substituting 8 oz. lobster meat for prawns.
Scallop rolls
As above, substituting 6 scallops (soaked in cold water for a few hours) for the lobster.
Shrimp rolls
As above, substituting an equivalent quantity of peeled shrimps for scallops.
Crab rolls
As above, substituting an equivalent quantity of crab meat for shrimps.
Oyster rolls
As above, substituting 1 dozen plump oysters for crab meat.

Shrimp patties
cooking time   5–6 minutes

you will need for 6 servings:

8 oz. fresh shrimps,	4 oz. spring onions,
shelled and cleaned	chopped
8 oz. fresh shoulder	1 teaspoon salt
of pork	½ teaspoon pepper
1 teaspoon lemon peel,	2 tablespoons cooking oil
grated	soya sauce

1 Cut the shrimps in pieces and pass through a mincer with pork, lemon peel, and spring onions.
2 The mixture should be very fine, so it is advisable to put it through the mincer two or even three times.
3 Season with salt and pepper.
4 Beat the mixture until perfectly blended, shape into round patties ½ inch thick.
5 Heat oil in pan, brown the patties on a moderate heat, pressing down with a fish slice to ensure that the pork cooks through.
6 Turn and brown the other side.
7 Serve hot with a small dish of soya sauce.

Butterfly shrimps

cooking time   9–10 minutes

you will need for 4–6 servings:

1½ lb. large fresh shrimps	4 tablespoons flour
2 egg whites	4–5 rashers lean bacon
½ teaspoon salt	2 tablespoons oil

1 Wash and shell the shrimps, rinse and drain.
2 Slash down the back of each shrimp with a sharp knife, remove the dark vein, then make a few slanting cuts on each shrimp.
3 Mix egg whites, salt, and flour.
4 Put a thin layer of this mixture into the long cut of each shrimp.
5 Cut the bacon rashers into pieces about 1½ inches across.
6 Put one of these bacon pieces on top of the egg white, salt, and flour mixture and press lightly with your palm.
7 Heat oil in a pan. Lay the shrimps bacon side down and cook until bacon is crisp.
8 Turn carefully to cook the other side.
9 As soon as the shrimps turn red, skewer them on cocktail sticks and serve in the sauce:

Sauce

cooking time   10 minutes

you will need for 4–6 servings:

2 small onions, finely chopped	½ pint chicken stock
1 teaspoon tomato purée	1 tablespoon cornflour
	3 tablespoons cold water

1 Fry the onions until golden in the fat left over from the shrimps.
2 Add tomato purée and chicken stock (bouillon made with boiling water and a chicken cube will do in an emergency).
3 Cook for two minutes, stirring constantly.
4 Mix cornflour with water, pour into the pan.
5 Blend in until the sauce thickens.

Shrimps and green peas

cooking time   5–6 minutes

you will need for 4–6 servings:

1 lb. shrimps, peeled (or prawns)	2 cloves garlic, crushed
1 tablespoon oil (peanut, if possible)	2 teaspoons cornflour
1 small packet frozen peas	3 tablespoons water
1 oz. ginger, finely chopped	½ teaspoon salt
1 oz. spring onion, finely chopped	1 teaspoon soya sauce
	pinch Ve-Tsin
	few drops sesame oil

1 Lightly fry the shrimps in oil for 1 minute. Remove from heat.
2 Boil the peas in salted water for 3 minutes and drain.
3 Combine shrimps, peas, ginger, onion and garlic in a frying pan. Stir well.
4 Dilute cornflour with 3 tablespoons cold water, mixed with salt, soya sauce and Ve-Tsin, and pour the mixture over the contents of the frying pan. Cook, stirring constantly, for 1–2 minutes, until the sauce thickens.
5 Sprinkle with sesame oil and serve.

Shrimps with corn noodles

cooking time   10 minutes

you will need for 4 servings:

2½ pints stock	½ teaspoon sugar
3 oz. dried shrimps	1 teaspoon soya sauce
2 oz. corn noodles	1 teaspoon dripping
½ teaspoon salt	few drops of sesame oil

1 Bring stock to the boil, add dried shrimps and cook for 5 minutes.
2 Add corn noodles and cook together for 3 minutes.
3 Add salt, sugar, soya sauce, dripping, and sesame oil.
4 Cook for 2 minutes, add more salt if necessary, and serve.

Shrimp kromeskis

cooking time   3–4 minutes

you will need for 4 servings:

1 lb. shrimps	1 teaspoon salt
4 oz. pork, minced	½ teaspoon sugar
4–6 water chestnuts, chopped	2 oz. plain flour
1 dessertspoon soya sauce	2 eggs beaten
	oil for deep frying

1 Shell and mince the shrimps.
2 Mix shrimps, pork, water chestnuts, soya sauce, salt, and sugar.
3 Shape into little balls, roll in flour, dip in egg and deep fry until golden.
4 Allow about 3 minutes cooking time. Drain and serve at once.

Variation

Sweet and sour shrimp pellets

Proceed as opposite, but instead of shaping the shrimp mixture into balls, take up a teaspoonful at a time and drop into boiling oil. Remove and drain as soon as they float up to the surface and turn golden. Heat sweet and sour sauce (see page 23), immerse pellets in it, and serve.

1 Clean the frogs' legs and keep in the refrigerator until required.
2 Break and remove the bone of each frog leg.
3 Cut the ham into thin strips and insert in each leg in the cavity left by the removal of the bone.
4 Beat the egg whites lightly, mix with flour and seasoning.
5 Dip the frogs' legs in this mixture, deep fry in oil until golden and crisp on the outside.
6 Serve hot with soya sauce or plum sauce. (See preceding recipe.)

Fan-tail shrimps

cooking time — 7–8 minutes

you will need for 4 servings:

1 lb. large fresh shrimps	½ teaspoon pepper
1 teaspoon sugar	1 egg, lightly beaten
1 oz. flour	oil for deep frying
½ teaspoon salt	1 red pepper, sliced

1 Wash and shell shrimps, leaving tail tips on. Remove dark vein, wash and drain.
2 Slit the middle, turn the tail up and pull through the slit.
3 Sift the sugar, flour, salt, and pepper together, and mix with the egg.
4 Dip the shrimps into this mixture, place in a frying basket and deep fry until golden.
5 Serve very hot with the garnish of red pepper and the sauce:

Plum sauce

cooking time — 5 minutes

you will need for 4 servings:

8 oz. plum jelly	1 tablespoon vinegar
4 oz. chutney, finely chopped	1 tablespoon sugar

1 Beat together all the ingredients indicated for plum sauce until smooth.
2 Serve separately in tiny dishes.

Stuffed frogs' legs

cooking time — 7–8 minutes

you will need for 4 servings:

1 lb. large frogs' legs	½ teaspoon salt
4 oz. lean ham	¼ teaspoon pepper
2 egg whites	oil for deep frying
2–3 tablespoons flour	

Frogs' legs with chicken livers

cooking time — 8 minutes

you will need for 4 servings:

1 tablespoon lard	4 oz. spring greens, shredded
1 teaspoon fresh ginger, cut in shreds	pinch salt
½ oz. spring onions, cut in 1-inch pieces	1 tablespoon soya sauce
12–16 frogs' legs, skinned and ready for cooking	1 teaspoon cornflour
	1 tablespoon Chinese wine (or sherry)
8 oz. chicken livers	pinch Ve-Tsin
2 oz. fresh mushrooms, sliced	½ teaspoon sugar

1 Heat lard in a pan, add ginger, spring onions and frogs' legs.
2 Cook for 2 minutes.
3 Add chicken livers, mushrooms, spring greens and cook for 1 minute, stirring constantly.
4 Add salt, soya sauce, cornflour diluted with wine, Ve-Tsin and sugar. Stir, simmer for 5 minutes and serve.

Frogs' legs with melon

cooking time — 25 minutes

you will need for 6 servings:

6 pairs frogs' legs, cut as above	1 oz. mushrooms, sliced
	stock to cover
½ teaspoon sugar	10–12 spring onions, cut in strips
1 teaspoon ginger root juice	1 teaspoon cornflour
1 teaspoon sherry	2 tablespoons cold water
salt	1 teaspoon sesame oil
2 lb. melon, diced	

1 Put leg pieces in hot oiled pan, add sugar, ginger root juice, sherry, salt to taste, and cook for 2 minutes.
2 Remove from pan, and cook melon for 2 minutes.
3 Add frogs' legs, mushrooms, and stock.
4 Simmer gently for 20 minutes. Add spring onions and cook for 1 minute.
5 Add cornflour diluted with water, sesame oil, and cook for 1 minute and serve.

Frogs' legs with pears

cooking time 7–8 minutes

you will need for 6 servings:

1½ lb. hard pears	salt
6 pairs frogs' legs	½ pint veal stock (or
1 dessertspoon oil	chicken stock)
1 teaspoon ginger root	1 teaspoon cornflour
juice	2–3 tablespoons cold
½ teaspoon sugar	water
1 teaspoon sherry	few drops sesame oil

1 Core and slice the pears.
2 Cut each frog's leg into 2 pieces and put in hot oiled pan together with ginger root juice, sugar, sherry, and salt to taste.
3 Cook for 2 minutes.
4 Remove frogs' legs and put in a dish.
5 Add pears to the pan and cook for 2 minutes.
6 Add frogs' legs and stock and cook together for 2 minutes. Add cornflour diluted with water, and sesame oil. Cook for 1 minute and serve.

Frogs' legs with tomatoes and green pimentos

cooking time 10 minutes

you will need for 6 servings:

6 pairs frogs' legs (cut	1–2 slices green ginger
as described in recipe	root, pounded
for Frogs' legs with	¾ pint hot, strained
pears, see above)	chicken stock (or water
2 large green pimentos	with chicken cube dis-
½ clove garlic, crushed	solved in it)
4 tablespoons cooking oil	2 tomatoes, quartered
½ teaspoon salt	2 tablespoons soya sauce
¼ teaspoon pepper	2 tablespoons cornflour
	2 tablespoons cold water
	3–4 spring onions,
	chopped

1 Toss the legs in a hot oiled pan for one minute and remove.
2 Wash and drain pimentos, cut into 6–8 pieces and discard seeds and fibres.
3 Heat the garlic, oil, salt, pepper, and ginger in the frying pan.
4 Add frogs' legs; cook for 3 minutes, stirring gently.
5 Add green peppers, mix, then add stock, stir well, cover, allow to come to the boil.
6 Simmer for 3–4 minutes, shaking the pan from time to time.
7 Add tomatoes, mix well, cook for 2–3 minutes.
8 Mix soya sauce, cornflour and water and pour into the pan.
9 Cook, stirring all the time, for 1–2 minutes, until the sauce thickens, add spring onions and serve.

Mullet Honan style

cooking time 18–20 minutes

you will need for 6 servings:

1 mullet (3 lb.) (or rock	6 tablespoons sugar
salmon)	6 tablespoons vinegar
2 tablespoons flour	2 tablespoons sherry
lard (or peanut oil) for	1 teaspoon salt
deep frying	3 tablespoons soya sauce
6 thin slices fresh ginger	3 tablespoons cornflour
2 shallots, sliced	¾ pint water
1 sweet pepper, seeded	
and shredded (red or	
green)	

1 Cut the fish into large portions, or leave whole and make several incisions on the back.
2 Sprinkle with flour and rub it in.
3 Deep fry for 10–15 minutes, depending on size of fish or portions. (A whole 3-lb. fish will need 15 minutes' cooking.)
4 Drain and arrange on a heated serving dish.
5 Pour off 1 tablespoon of the fat into a saucepan and lightly fry ginger and shallots for 1 minute. Add sweet pepper, cook for 1 minute.
6 Sprinkle in sugar, vinegar, sherry, salt and soya sauce. Stir.
7 Gradually dilute cornflour with water and blend into the sauce.
8 Cook for 1–2 minutes, until the sauce thickens and becomes translucent.
9 Pour sauce over the fish and serve.

Plaice rolls with ham and almond stuffing

cooking time 5 minutes

you will need for 6 servings:

1 lb. plaice fillets,	1 teaspoon sugar
skinned	1 teaspoon cornflour
1 teaspoon salt	1 egg, beaten
2 teaspoons soya sauce	oil (or lard) for deep
pinch Ve-Tsin	frying
1 teaspoon fresh ginger	2 doz. blanched, roasted
juice	almonds
1 teaspoon onion juice	2 oz. ham, smoked, in
1 teaspoon Chinese wine	thin slices
(or sherry)	

1 Cut the fillets into oblongs measuring 2-inches by 3-inches.
2 Put in a dish, sprinkle with salt, soya sauce and Ve-Tsin.
3 Mix ginger and onion juice, wine, sugar, cornflour and egg. Pour this dressing over the fish, mix well.
4 Put fat to heat.
5 In a mortar grind almonds into a paste.
6 Cut ham slices into 2-inch strips.
7 Spread fish slices with almond paste, cover this filling with a strip of ham, roll up the fillets and either seal up with egg or secure with a cocktail stick.
8 Deep fry the stuffed plaice rolls for 4–5 minutes, drain, remove cocktail sticks (if used) and serve at once.

Eggs

Eggs, along with vegetables, play an important part in the Chinese diet. In addition to various egg dishes, the recipes for which are given below, the Chinese are also very fond of preserved eggs. Salted duck eggs (Hahm Dahn) are sold ready for the table and only require shelling and cutting into quarters. No section on Chinese egg dishes will be complete without the mention of 'hundred-year-old eggs' (Pay Dahn). This is a much-maligned delicacy, like oysters and caviar, an acquired taste but well worth the acquisition. The process of preserving normally takes from two to three months. The eggs are no more 'rotten' than the English waterglass egg, but the difference in the method produces a different result. They are served cut up into segments and make an excellent hors-d'oeuvre, usually served with Chinese pickles.

Steamed eggs

cooking time   15 minutes

you will need for 4 servings:

3 eggs	1 teaspoon salt
¼ pint milk	½ pint water
1 dessertspoon oil (or butter)	

1 Beat the eggs, add milk, oil, salt, and water.
2 Whisk together in a bowl, then place the bowl in a steamer with a well fitting lid.
3 Steam for 15 minutes.

Note:

This dish should have the consistency of a custard.

Steamed egg and plaice fillets

cooking time   30 minutes

you will need for 6 servings:

1 lb. plaice fillets	2 tablespoons oil
4 eggs	1 tablespoon lemon peel, shredded
¼ pint water	
1 teaspoon salt	3 spring onions, chopped
½ teaspoon pepper	soya sauce

1 Mince the fish fillets.
2 Beat the eggs with the water.
3 Add fish with salt, pepper, oil, and lemon peel.
4 Spread on a dish set on a rack in a pan of boiling water (the water to reach to within 1 inch of the rack).
5 Cover the pan, bring water to boil and steam for 30 minutes.
6 Sprinkle with spring onions and soya sauce and serve.

Steamed eggs with bacon

cooking time   15 minutes

you will need for 4—6 servings:

4—6 eggs	½ teaspoon salt
3 tablespoons water	3—4 spring onions, chopped
4 oz. bacon, chopped	
1 dessertspoon soya sauce	

1 Beat the eggs with water.
2 Add the rest of the ingredients.
3 Pour into a basin, or into individual ramekin dishes.
4 Steam for 15 minutes and serve.

Variations:

Steamed eggs with pork
As above, substituting 4 oz. lean pork, minced, for bacon.

Steamed eggs with prawns
As above, substituting 4 oz. peeled prawns for pork.

Steamed eggs with shrimps
As above, substituting 4 oz. peeled shrimps for prawns.

Steamed eggs with mushrooms
As above, substituting 4 oz. mushrooms, chopped, for shrimps.

Steamed eggs with ham and bamboo shoots
As above, substituting 4 oz. lean ham, diced and 2 oz. bamboo shoots, sliced, for mushrooms.

Shredded egg (garnish)

cooking time   5–6 minutes

you will need:

1 egg, well-beaten
little oil

1 Grease a hot frying pan with just enough oil to cover the bottom.
2 Pour in a little of the egg in a thin pancake.
3 Cook slowly for 2½–3 minutes.
4 Turn out, fold and cut into very fine shreds.
5 Repeat until all egg is used. Use as garnish for soups.

Scrambled eggs with spring onions

cooking time   6–7 minutes

you will need for 4 servings:

3 eggs
4 oz. spring onions, chopped
2 rashers bacon, shredded
1 teaspoon orange zest, grated
1 teaspoon salt
2 tablespoons oil

1 Beat the eggs.
2 Add spring onions, bacon, and orange zest.
3 Season with salt.
4 Heat oil, pour in the egg mixture.
5 Scramble gently on a low heat until it acquires a creamy consistency.

Braised eggs

cooking time   14 minutes

you will need for 4 servings:

4 eggs
3 tablespoons soya sauce
1 tablespoon oil

1 Boil eggs for 4 minutes, put under running cold water for 5 minutes.
2 Shell, wipe and put in small saucepan with soya sauce and oil.
3 Braise gently for 5 minutes, basting frequently, until they turn brown.
4 Leave to get cold. Cut into quarters and serve.

Eggs with spinach

cooking time   5 minutes

you will need for 4 servings:

4 oz. leaf spinach
1 tablespoon oil
3 eggs, beaten
salt and pepper

1 Wash spinach, shake out and fry briskly for 3 minutes in oil.
2 Remove from pan.
3 Chop the spinach, add to eggs, season with salt and pepper and whisk together.

4 Reheat the pan, making sure that the whole of the bottom of it is greased.
5 Pour in egg and spinach mixture.
6 Fry for 2–3 minutes.

Eggs and crab

cooking time   5 minutes

you will need for 6 servings:

8 oz. cooked (or canned) crab meat
8 oz. fresh bean sprouts
2 tablespoons oil
1½ teaspoons salt
½ teaspoon pepper
6 eggs
3–4 spring onions

1 Pick over the crab meat, discarding any cartilage.
2 Wash and drain bean sprouts.
3 Heat oil and toss the crab meat for 1 minute.
4 Add bean sprouts, season with salt and pepper, mix and cook for 1 minute.
5 Beat the eggs lightly and stir carefully into the mixture.
6 Cook on low heat, stir once or twice, but do not scramble.
7 Scatter the spring onions over the top, serve as soon as the eggs are set.

Eggs and scallops

cooking time   7–8 minutes

you will need for 4–6 servings:

1 lb. small fresh scallops
5 tablespoons cooking oil
1 teaspoon salt
¼ teaspoon pepper
4 oz. onions, chopped
1 tablespoon soya sauce
4 eggs
3–4 spring onions, chopped

1 Cut the scallops into pieces.
2 Heat the oil and sprinkle salt and pepper into it.
3 Add onion and cook until transparent.
4 Add scallops, stir and cook uncovered on low heat for 2–3 minutes.
5 Sprinkle with soya sauce.
6 Beat the eggs lightly, mix with spring onions, pour over scallops.
7 Cook until the eggs are set and serve.

Pork or ham Foo Yung

cooking time   5 minutes

you will need for 6 servings:

6 oz. ham (or pork) shredded
3 tablespoons lard
6–8 spring onions, shredded
6 eggs
2 tablespoons light coloured soya sauce
2 oz. bean sprouts, washed
1 teaspoon cornflour
3–4 tablespoons cold water

1 Fry pork (or ham) in 1 tablespoon lard for 1 minute.
2 Add spring onions, fry for 1 minute, stirring constantly and remove from heat.
3 Heat remaining lard in another frying pan.
4 Beat eggs with soya sauce and 1 tablespoon cold water.
5 Add fried contents and bean sprouts and fry the mixture as a thick pancake, $1\frac{1}{2}$ minutes each side, turning once to brown both sides.
6 Put on a heated serving dish, cut into wedges and keep warm.
7 Blend cornflour with water, stir into the pan juices, bring to the boil, cook until the sauce thickens, pour over the Foo Yung and serve.

Variation

Chicken Foo Yung
Follow recipe for Pork or ham Foo Yung, but substitute equivalent amount of raw chicken, shredded, for pork, and celery, shredded, for bean sprouts.

Shrimp Foo Yung

cooking time   4–5 minutes

you will need for 4 servings:

2 tablespoons lard	4 eggs
4 oz. shrimps, peeled	cold water
2 tablespoons light coloured soya sauce	pinch salt
2 oz. celery, shredded	2 oz. bean sprouts, washed
1 medium-sized onion, chopped	1 teaspoon cornflour

1 Heat 1 tablespoon lard and fry shrimps for 1 minute.
2 Add soya sauce, celery and onion. Cook for 1 minute, stirring constantly. Remove from heat.
3 In another frying pan, heat the rest of the lard.
4 Beat the eggs lightly with 1 tablespoon cold water and the salt.
5 Pour into hot lard, cook the eggs, *without stirring,* for a few seconds, until they begin to set.
6 Pile shrimp and vegetable mixture and the bean sprouts on one half of the eggs, fold to enclose the filling. Cook for 1 minute.
7 Turn carefully, cook for 1 minute and transfer to a heated serving plate. Keep warm.
8 Dilute the juices left in the pan from frying shrimps etc. with $\frac{1}{4}$ pint water.
9 Blend cornflour with 2 tablespoons cold water, stir into the pan juices, bring to the boil, simmer for a few seconds until the sauce becomes thick and translucent.
10 Pour over the Foo Yung and serve.

Conference omelette

cooking time   20–25 minutes

you will need for 4–6 servings:

6–8 eggs, well beaten	1 dessertspoon peanut oil
2 dozen oysters, chopped	salt
3 oz. fat pork, minced	6 water chestnuts, finely sliced
6 olives, stoned and shredded	1 oz. shrimps, chopped
2 spring onions, chopped	little water
1 dessertspoon soya sauce.	

1 Put all the ingredients in a big bowl, mix and add a little water as for a custard (decreasing it if the oysters give out a lot of liquid).
2 Pour the mixture into a dish and either steam or bake it until it sets.
3 Serve at once.

Prawn and vegetable omelette

cooking time $3\frac{1}{2}$ minutes

you will need for 6 servings:

1 dessertspoon oil	$\frac{1}{2}$ oz. onions, chopped
2 oz. prawns, peeled and diced	1 oz. mushrooms, finely sliced
$1\frac{1}{2}$ oz. chicken, diced	salt and pepper
$1\frac{1}{2}$ oz. ham, diced	6 eggs, beaten

1 Heat a pan and put all ingredients in it except eggs. Cook for 2 minutes.
2 Season with salt and pepper.
3 Add eggs. Cook for $1\frac{1}{2}$ minutes and serve.

Variation

Omelette with bamboo shoots and bean sprouts
As above, omitting prawns, chicken, ham and mushrooms, but allowing 3 oz. each of bamboo shoots, sliced, and bean sprouts.

Minced pork omelette

cooking time   7 minutes

you will need for 6 servings:

1 dessertspoon oil	6 eggs, beaten
1 oz. onions, chopped	salt and pepper
6 oz. pork, minced	

1 Heat oil in pan and cook onions for 30 seconds.
2 Add pork and cook together gently for 5 minutes.
3 Season the eggs with salt and pepper.
4 Pour over the pork and onion mixture and cook together for $1\frac{1}{2}$ minutes.
5 Shake the pan to ensure even cooking, and serve.

Oyster omelette (1)

cooking time   5–6 minutes

you will need for 4–6 servings:

4 eggs	2 oz. fresh mushrooms,
½ pint milk	sliced
½ teaspoon Ve-Tsin	1 oz. bamboo shoots,
salt	sliced
1½ dozen plump oysters	½ oz. spring onions,
1 dessertspoon oil	finely chopped
2 oz. lean, uncooked pork	pepper

1 Beat the eggs, add milk, Ve-Tsin, salt and oysters.
2 Heat oil in pan.
3 While heating, shred the pork, then quick fry it in the oil.
4 As soon as it turns uniformly white, add mushrooms and bamboo shoots. Cook for 1 minute.
5 Add spring onions to the egg mixture.
6 Season with pepper, pour into the pan and fold in the usual way, and serve with the following sauce poured over it.

Sauce

cooking time   5 minutes

you will need for 4–6 servings:

1 dessertspoon oyster	1 teaspoon cornflour
sauce	2 tablespoons cold water
1 teaspoon soya sauce	

1 Combine oyster sauce, soya sauce and cornflour diluted with water.
2 Reduce sauce a little to thicken, and serve.

Variation

Mussel omelette
As above, substituting mussels for oysters.

Oyster omelette (2)

As recipe for Shredded pork omelette, see page 73, substituting 1½ dozen plump oysters for the shredded pork. It is usual to serve this with a sauce.

Sauce

cooking time   5 minutes

you will need for 4 servings:

1 dessertspoon oyster	1 teaspoon cornflour
sauce	1 teaspoon soya sauce
¼ pint water	

1 Combine all the ingredients, cook till thick.
2 Pour over the omelette and serve.

Ham and pea omelette

cooking time   7–8 minutes

you will need for 4 servings:

8 oz. peas, shelled	1 teaspoon soya sauce
salted water	1 teaspoon salt
1 tablespoon oil	pepper
4 oz. lean ham, shredded	10 chives, chopped
4 eggs	

1 Boil peas quickly in water for about 4 minutes and strain.
2 Quick fry the ham in a lightly greased pan (1 minute).
3 Whisk eggs in a basin with soya sauce, salt, pepper and chives.
4 Allow ham to cool, then add to the eggs with the peas.
5 Whisk together, then fry in the ordinary way in a hot oiled pan.

Note:
Do not over-cook.

Variations
Bacon and bean omelette
As above, substituting bacon for ham and sliced beans for peas.
Bacon and bean sprout omelette
As above, substituting bean sprouts for beans, but do not boil the bean sprouts; simply toss them in the pan with the bacon.

Scrambled eggs with dried shrimps and cod fillet

cooking time   5 minutes

you will need for 6 servings:

1½ oz. shrimps, dried	1 teaspoon salt
1½ pints water	2½ oz. flour
6 eggs	3 tablespoons peanut oil
8 oz. cod fillet, diced	

1 Bring the shrimps to the boil in just enough water to cover.
2 As soon as boiling is established, remove from heat, leave, covered, for 25 minutes, then drain but keep the liquid.
3 Beat the eggs with the shrimp, shrimp liquid, cod and salt.
4 Gradually dilute flour with remaining water and stir it into the egg mixture.
5 Beat together to amalgamate all ingredients.
6 Heat the oil, pour the eggs in, scramble quickly and serve at once.

Shredded pork omelette

cooking time   6–7 minutes

you will need for 4 servings:

1 dessertspoon oil	10 chives, chopped
4 oz. raw pork, shredded	salt and pepper
4 oz. mushrooms, finely	½ pint milk
sliced	¼ teaspoon Ve-Tsin
1 oz. bamboo shoots,	4 eggs, beaten
finely sliced	

1 Heat oil in pan and fry the pork for 4–5 minutes.
2 Add mushrooms, bamboo shoots, chives and salt and pepper to taste.
3 Cook for 1 minute.
4 Add milk and Ve-Tsin to eggs and pour mixture into the pan.
5 Cook for 1 minute and serve.

Variation

Pork and tomato omelette

As for bacon and bean sprout omelette page 72, substituting 4 oz. pork minced for bacon and 4 oz. peeled tomatoes for bean sprouts.

Chrysanthemum omelette

cooking time   1 minute per 'chrysanthemum'

you will need for 4 servings:

4 eggs	2 tablespoons lard
pinch salt	strip of red pimento
pinch Ve-Tsin	

1 Beat the eggs lightly, season with salt and Ve-Tsin.
2 Heat omelette pan, grease lightly and use just enough egg mixture to make a film on the bottom of the pan.
3 Fry these paper-thin pancake omelettes, until all the mixture is used up.
4 Lift the omelettes from the pan to a cutting board and cut into 3-inch by 6-inch strips.
5 Fold over once, make 1-inch incisions downwards through the double thickness.
6 Roll into a cylinder and open out the cut to form a 'chrysanthemum'.
7 Stamp out a small circle of red pimento (or tomato) and put in the centre of each flower.

Note:

This tastes good and looks very decorative with a green salad.

Rice, Noodles, Egg Rolls and Patties

Rice, the staple food of the Chinese, occupies roughly the same place in the Chinese scheme of things as bread does, say, in France. It is indispensable, but the richer one is the less one needs of it. The appearance of cooked rice is considered to be of great importance. If cooked correctly, and this is mainly a question of observing the right proportions of rice to water, the grains should be firm and separate. Rice should be washed thoroughly before cooking. Our cook in China used to say 'in nine waters', and the last water poured off should be completely clear.

Noodles are almost equally important as a staple food. They are eaten as a main course. People will often have a bowl of noodle soup or a dish of braised noodles for lunch or supper—and delicious they are too. Noodles also play a traditional part on special occasions, particularly at birthday dinners, because they are a symbol of long life. When serving noodles, never cut them, for that 'shortens the life'.

Plain boiled rice (1)

cooking time   20 minutes

you will need for 4 servings:

1 lb. rice	1½ pints water

1 Wash the rice thoroughly until the water is clear. (The amount of water required varies with the quality of rice. The thing to remember is that the better the quality of rice, the less water it needs.)
2 Put rice and water in a thick saucepan, cover as soon as boiling is established.
3 Leave undisturbed to simmer for 20 minutes.

Plain boiled rice (2)

cooking time   18–20 minutes

you will need for 4 servings:

8 oz. rice	water

1 Put the rice into a fairly broad saucepan and cover with water, allowing 'two fingers', i.e. 1-inch of water above the level of the rice.
2 Bring to the boil and allow to boil fast until the water is absorbed.
3 Cover with a lid, reduce heat to the minimum and leave to simmer for 12 minutes.

Plain boiled rice (3)

cooking time   18–20 minutes

you will need for 4 servings:

8 oz. rice	¾ pint cold water

1 Wash the rice in water several times.
2 Add water, cover and boil over a hot flame until the water evaporates. Do not stir while rice is boiling, as this will prevent the grains from separating.
3 Keep warm until ready for use, leaving the lid on. (If an electric stove is used, heat may be turned off and pot kept covered on the burner. If the rice is cooked on a gas stove, turn the flame down very low after the water has evaporated.)

Note:

Roughly speaking, 8 oz. uncooked rice makes double that quantity cooked rice.

Rice with mushrooms

cooking time   25 minutes

you will need for 4 servings:

8 oz. rice	2 tablespoons cold water
1 tablespoon oil (or butter)	2 oz. meat (lean beef, veal or pork), sliced
1 teaspoon salt	1 teaspoon soya sauce
8 oz. mushrooms, sliced	
1 teaspoon cornflour	

1 Boil the rice as described, adding ½ teaspoon oil and salt.
2 Fry mushrooms lightly in the remaining oil and add cornflour diluted with water.
3 Add meat to the mushrooms.
4 Season with soya sauce, toss together for a few minutes, and pile all these ingredients on top of the rice when the latter has absorbed nearly all the water.
5 Cover, and simmer gently for 15 minutes.

Rice and steamed chicken

cooking time   25 minutes

you will need for 4 servings:

4 oz. chicken, sliced	10 chives, chopped
4 oz. mushrooms, sliced	1 tablespoon cornflour
1 oz. celery, diced	1 tablespoon soya sauce
1 oz. bamboo shoots, diced	8 oz. rice
	1 tablespoon butter

1 Mix chicken and vegetables with cornflour and soya sauce.
2 Boil the rice, and when water is nearly absorbed pile the chicken and vegetables on top of it with the butter.
3 Cover. Simmer gently for 15 minutes.

Note:

This will be enough to cook the chicken and for it to impart its flavour to the rice.

Boiled rice with chicken and oyster sauce

cooking time   25 minutes

you will need for 4 servings:

6 oz. raw chicken, shredded	8 oz. rice
1 teaspoon salt	3 oz. mushrooms, sliced
1 teaspoon soya sauce	1 tablespoon chives, chopped
1 teaspoon brandy	1 dessertspoon oyster sauce
1 teaspoon cornflour	

1 Season the chicken with salt, mix with soya sauce, brandy and cornflour.
2 Start cooking the rice in the ordinary way, until it has absorbed almost all the water.
3 Pile the chicken and the mushrooms on top of it and simmer for 15 minutes.
4 Sprinkle with chives, add oyster sauce, stir and serve.

Boiled rice with chicken and tomatoes

cooking time   25 minutes

you will need for 4 servings:

1 lb. rice	4 oz. tomatoes, peeled
1 dessertspoon oil	and quartered
1 clove garlic, crushed	1 teaspoon sugar
6 oz. raw chicken,	salt and pepper
shredded	1 tablespoon spring
	onions, chopped

1 Start boiling the rice in the ordinary way.
2 Heat oil with garlic and quickly toss in the chicken and the tomatoes.
3 Add sugar, and salt and pepper to taste, and simmer until chicken is cooked and tomatoes reduced to pulp.
4 Pile this mixture on top of the rice when the latter has absorbed almost all the water.
5 Sprinkle with spring onions, cover, simmer for 15 minutes and serve.

Fried rice (1)

cooking time   6–7 minutes

you will need for 4 servings:

1 tablespoon lard (or oil)	few spring onions,
1 lb. rice, cooked	chopped
2 eggs, beaten	1 dessertspoon soya sauce

1 Heat lard in a pan.
2 Fry the rice in it quickly, stirring all the time.
3 Pour eggs over the rice, fry slowly together for 4–5 minutes.
4 Sprinkle with spring onions, season with soya sauce and serve.

Note:

Boiled rice is the best to use for fried rice dishes because it has the right consistency.

Fried rice (2)

cooking time   5–6 minutes

you will need for 4–6 servings:

2 tablespoons oil	1 lb. cooked meat,
1 lb. onions, chopped	chopped
8 oz. rice, cooked, cold	1 green pimento, chopped
2 eggs, lightly beaten	2 tablespoons peanuts,
1 tablespoon soya sauce	shelled and roasted
½ teaspoon salt	

1 Heat pan, add oil, fry onions until golden.
2 Add rice and cook together, stirring well.
3 Add eggs, soya sauce and salt. Cook, stirring, until the eggs are done.
4 Add chopped meat, pimento and peanuts.
5 Cook until meat is heated through and serve.

Fried rice with ham and beans

cooking time   5–6 minutes

you will need for 4 servings:

2 eggs, beaten	4 oz. beans, sliced
salt and pepper	1 tablespoon soya sauce
2 tablespoons oil	1 lb. cooked cold rice
4 oz. ham, shredded	3–4 spring onions,
1 small onion, chopped	chopped

1 Season eggs with salt and pepper to taste and cook as an ordinary omelette in a lightly greased pan.
2 Remove and keep hot.
3 Quick fry the ham with onions and beans for about 20 seconds, stirring all the time.
4 Season with soya sauce and simmer for 3 minutes.
5 Add rice, breaking it down with chopsticks to loosen the grains and to heat it through.
6 Slice the omelette, scatter over the rice, sprinkle with spring onions and serve.

Variations

Fried rice with chicken
As above, substituting 8 oz. chicken meat, sliced, for ham and beans.
Fried rice with pork
As above, substituting 8 oz. roast pork, diced, for chicken.
Subgum fried rice
Follow recipe for Fried rice with chicken (see above), adding to the mixture 2 oz. fresh or canned mushrooms, diced, 2 oz. pimento, diced, 2 oz. water chestnuts, diced. If desired, meat, fish or shellfish can be used instead of chicken.
Fried rice with prawns
As above, substituting 6–8 oz. fresh prawns, sliced, for chicken.
Fried rice with lobster
As above, substituting lobster, diced, for prawns.
Fried rice with crab
As above, substituting crab meat for lobster.
Fried rice with shrimps and ham
As above, substituting 2 oz. fresh shrimps and 2 oz. ham for crab meat.
Vegetable fried rice
Omit ham and beans in Fried rice with ham and beans (see above), adding a garnish of red and green pepper, sliced and instead add any available vegetable: 2 pimentos, diced fresh, 1 canned pimento, diced, 4 oz. bean sprouts, 8 oz. carrots, diced. The proportion of ingredients in vegetable fried rice dishes should be twice as much cooked rice as mixed vegetables.

Boiled mixed rice

cooking time   25 minutes

you will need for 4 servings:

1 lb. rice	4 oz. peas, shelled
4 oz. pork, shredded	1 dessertspoon oyster
1 teaspoon salt	sauce
1 dessertspoon soya sauce	1 tablespoon spring
1 teaspoon brandy	onions, chopped
1 teaspoon cornflour	1–2 eggs, scrambled
1–2 Chinese sausages	
(Lap Cheong)	

1 Start boiling the rice in the ordinary way.
2 Season pork with salt and soya sauce, sprinkle with brandy and dredge with cornflour.
3 Blanch the sausages and cut into small pieces.
4 When the rice has absorbed almost all the water, pile on top of it pork, sausages and peas.
5 Cover and simmer for 15 minutes, then add oyster sauce and spring onions, stir.
6 Garnish with thin slices of egg and serve.

Beef and rice

cooking time   8–10 minutes

you will need for 4 servings:

12 oz.–1 lb. hot rice,	½ pint boiling water
freshly cooked	3–4 spring onions, cut
3 tablespoons cooking oil	in 1½-inch pieces
1 small clove garlic	4 oz. fresh mushrooms,
½ teaspoon salt	sliced
¼ teaspoon pepper	2 tablespoons cornflour
1 lb. beef, minced	4 tablespoons cold water
3 tablespoons soya sauce	4 eggs

1 As soon as the rice is ready, heat the oil, crush the garlic into it, add salt and pepper and quick fry the beef for 3 minutes.
2 Add soya sauce, water, spring onions and mushrooms.
3 Bring to the boil, then simmer, stirring continually for 3 minutes.
4 Mix cornflour with water and blend into the pan to thicken the sauce.
5 Transfer the rice into a big casserole or into 4 individual dishes, pour sauce over the rice.
6 With a spoon make a 'nest' in the centre of the rice (4 'nests' if serving in one large casserole), break an egg into each 'nest', cover at once, allow the eggs to cook in the hot rice and sauce until set and serve.

Variation:

Curried beef and rice Cantonese style
Add 2 tablespoons curry powder to the hot pan in which the meat is cooked, then proceed as described in the recipe above.

Fried rice with pork and shredded omelette

cooking time   8–10 minutes

you will need for 4 servings:

2 cups cooked rice	4 oz. bean sprouts
(see page 74)	2 eggs
12 oz. lean pork	pinch salt
3–4 tablespoons peanut oil	1 teaspoon lukewarm
4 spring onions, chopped	water
1 clove garlic, chopped	1 tablespoon soya sauce

1 Leave the rice to cool.
2 Cut pork into very thin slices and fry it in oil until it turns pale.
3 Move to the side of the pan, and fry spring onions and garlic for 2 minutes.
4 Add bean sprouts and simmer together for 2 minutes.
5 Beat eggs with salt and water and in a separate pan fry an omelette.
6 Cut it into thin strips.
7 Add rice to the pork, fry long enough only to heat through the rice (2 minutes), season with soya sauce, stir well.
8 Transfer fried rice to a heated serving dish, garnish with shredded omelette and serve.

Most precious rice

cooking time   6–7 minutes

you will need for 6–8 servings:

8 oz. lean pork (or	1 tablespoon spring
chicken)	onions, chopped
8 oz. peas (or beans),	2–3 eggs
shelled	1 dessertspoon soya
4 oz. prawns (or crab	sauce
meat), peeled	oil
4 oz. mushrooms, sliced	1½–2 lb. cold rice,
2 oz. bamboo shoots,	cooked
diced	

1 See that all ingredients are cut to a uniform size, determining the size and shape by the smallest natural ingredient; thus, if peas are used, the rest of the ingredients must be cut into dice no bigger than a pea.
2 Beat eggs with soya sauce and keep by.
3 Cook all other ingredients in a deep oiled pan, season to taste, add rice, stirring until it becomes separate and quite hot.
4 Stir to mix well. Pour the eggs over the whole mixture.
5 Increase heat to cook quickly and keep stirring until the eggs have been integrated into the mixture and are quite dry.

Chicken noodles

cooking time   25 minutes

you will need for 4 servings:

4 tablespoons oil (or chicken fat)
3 teaspoons salt
¼ teaspoon pepper
8 oz. Chinese cabbage, sliced
8 oz. celery, shredded
4 oz. bean sprouts, washed and drained
2 teaspoons sugar
1 pint chicken stock (or water with a chicken cube dissolved in it)

4 tablespoons soya sauce
2½ tablespoons cornflour
2 tablespoons cold water
1 lb. cooked chicken, sliced (or shredded fresh chicken)
8 oz. thin noodles, fried
2 eggs, chopped, hard-boiled

To fry thin noodles:
Drop them into boiling water, drain at once, put in a colander, place over pan of boiling water and steam for 20 minutes. Drain. Pan-fry in hot oil or deep fry till crisp. Drain and use as described.

1 Heat oil, salt and pepper and add all the vegetables, bean sprouts last of all.
2 Sprinkle in sugar, stir.
3 Add stock, mix well and cover with a lid.
4 Bring to the boil, stir well, cover and simmer for 10 minutes.
5 Mix soya sauce, cornflour and water and blend into the vegetables.
6 Stir until the sauce thickens. Add chicken, cook for 1–2 minutes.
7 Place fried noodles on a large dish, or on four individual dishes.
8 Cover noodles with vegetable and chicken mixture, top with eggs and serve.

Variations:

Noodles with almonds
Follow recipe for Chicken noodles (see above) but substitute 4 oz. chopped almonds as a topping instead of chopped hard-boiled egg.

Noodles with shrimps
Follow recipe for Chicken noodles (see above) but substitute 8 oz. cooked or canned shrimps, diced, for the chicken.

'Ten Varieties of Beauty'
This is an elaboration of Chicken noodles (see above) but must include ten different vegetables, such as water chestnuts, bamboo shoots, celery, mushrooms, pimentos, French beans, onions, almonds, cabbage, cauliflower, as well as the noodles and chicken, meat or shellfish and the sauce.

Fried noodles

cooking time   20 minutes

you will need for 4 servings:

1 lb. noodles
water
4 oz. lard (or oil)
4 oz. lean pork, sliced
4 oz. Chinese white cabbage

2 oz. celery, diced
2 oz. mushrooms, sliced
1 oz. bamboo shoots, sliced
1 tablespoon soya sauce

1 Boil noodles for 5 minutes in 3 pints water as described in Chicken noodles. (As soon as they float to the surface they are ready.)
2 Rinse under cold tap, drain well and spread on a dish.
3 Heat lard and cook meat and vegetables in it for 5 minutes, stirring briskly all the time.
4 Add soya sauce and mix.
5 Fry the noodles separately in 2 tablespoons oil for 5 minutes.
6 Add cooked vegetables and meat, fry together for 5 minutes, taste for seasoning and add more soya sauce if required, and serve.

Variations:

Fried noodles with mixed vegetables
As in recipe above, substituting 3 oz. bean sprouts, 1 oz. spring onions, chopped, 4 oz. beans and 4 oz. ham, shredded, for the meat and vegetables given.

Fried noodles with chicken and mushrooms
As above, allowing 6 oz. chicken meat, diced, and 3 oz. mushrooms, sliced, in place of the meat and vegetables given.

Fried noodles with crab
Proceed as in previous recipe, allowing 5 oz. crab meat, 2 oz. chopped onion, 1 oz. bamboo shoots, finely sliced, 2 oz. mushrooms, sliced, and 4 oz. bean sprouts in place of the chicken and mushrooms.

Fried noodles with chicken and broccoli
This is a very famous dish which Marco Polo introduced to Europe and which was the forefather of all pasta. There are many varieties of this recipe. The simplest one is to proceed as above, allowing 8 oz. broccoli to 1 lb. noodles, and 8 oz. chicken, diced. A teaspoon of finely pounded ginger is added to the chicken.

Fresh noodles

cooking time   5 minutes

you will need for 4 servings:

1 lb. flour   2 eggs
½ teaspoon salt

1 Using 12 oz. flour, salt and eggs, make a dough.
2 Knead well and roll out thinly. (To ensure evenness of rolling out, always roll forward.)
3 Use the rest of the flour for sprinkling the pastry board to prevent sticking.
4 Fold the dough and cut into strips – fine ones for soup, wider ones for braising, frying, etc.
5 Sprinkle a little flour over the strips and loosen them out on a board into long strips. (If not using immediately, cover with a damp cloth.)
6 Allow 3 pints of water to boil 1 lb. of noodles, and always put the noodles into boiling water, separating them with a pair of chopsticks to prevent sticking.

Crispy noodles

cooking time   12–13 minutes

you will need for 4 servings:

1 lb. fresh egg noodles   2 oz. onions, chopped
1 lb. lard (or oil)   8 oz. lean pork
4 oz. white cabbage   1 tablespoon soya sauce

1 Boil noodles for 5 minutes, rinse under cold water tap and drain well.
2 Melt the fat, arrange the noodles in a strainer or frying basket and deep fry for 5 minutes until crispy and golden. Remove.
3 Chop the vegetables and meat finely, fry together for a few minutes in a tablespoon of hot lard. Add soya sauce and serve on top of the crispy noodles.

Noodles with shredded chicken

cooking time   15–16 minutes

you will need for 4 servings:

2 oz. dried Chinese   3 spring onions, chopped
   mushrooms   1 lb. cooked chicken,
4 oz. Chinese noodles   shredded
peanut oil for deep   pinch salt
   frying   2 tablespoons soya sauce
1 onion, chopped

1 Soak the mushrooms in enough warm water to cover for 20 minutes.
2 Drain and remove stalks. Slice the mushrooms.
3 Boil noodles in plenty of salted water for 5 minutes, drain and rinse with cold water. Drain well.
4 Heat oil and deep fry noodles until crisp and golden. This should take about 3–4 minutes. Remove, arrange on a serving dish and keep warm.
5 Pour off most of the fat, leaving 1–2 tablespoons in the pan and fry the onions for 1 minute.
6 Add chicken, fry for 1 minute. Season with salt and soya sauce.
7 Add mushrooms, fry together for 5 minutes, stirring all the time.
8 Spoon the chicken and mushroom garnish on top of the noodles and serve.

Crispy noodles with chicken and bamboo shoots

cooking time   13 minutes

you will need for 4 servings:

1 lb. fresh egg noodles   2 oz. mushrooms, diced
4 oz. chicken meat, diced   1 medium-size onion,
oil for deep frying   chopped
salt and pepper   1 teaspoon cornflour
2 oz. bamboo shoots, sliced   2 tablespoons cold water
6 oz. bean sprouts   1 dessertspoon soya sauce
                     few drops of sesame oil

1 Cook noodles as preceding recipe.
2 After deep frying put in a serving dish and keep hot (pressing noodles to sides of the frying basket, this helps to make them into a 'nest').
3 Cook chicken in a hot oiled pan for 1 minute.
4 Season with salt and pepper to taste.
5 Add bamboo shoots, bean sprouts, mushrooms and onion and cook for 1 minute.
6 Add cornflour, diluted with water and soya sauce and cook for 1 minute.
7 Sprinkle with sesame oil and serve the whole on top of the noodles.

Variations

Crispy noodles with crab, lobster or prawn
Any one of the above may be substituted for the chicken.
Crispy noodles with pork and water chestnuts
Proceed as described in the recipe for Crispy noodles with chicken and bamboo shoots, substituting chicken and bamboo shoots by 6 oz. pork, minced and 4 oz. water chestnuts, shredded.

Spring rolls

cooking time   30–35 minutes

you will need for 4 servings:

8 oz. pork, minced   1 dessertspoon soya sauce
few spring onions,   salt and pepper
   chopped   1 slice fresh ginger,
8 oz. bean sprouts   crushed
oil   batter, see page 79

1 Mix the pork with onions and bean sprouts and fry in oil for 5 minutes.
2 Add soya sauce, season with salt and pepper and ginger, cook for another 3 minutes. Leave to cool.
3 Then proceed to make rolls as described in the recipe for Pancake rolls, (see below), deep fry, drain and serve.

Variation

Stuff the pancakes with a mixture composed of 8 oz. pork, minced, 4 oz. prawns, peeled, chopped, 4 oz. cabbage, shredded, and 2 oz. celery, diced, with a tablespoon of spring onions, chopped, and ½ teaspoon of Ve-Tsin.

Braised noodles

cooking time   18–20 minutes

you will need for 4 servings:

1 lb. noodles	8 oz. lean pork
1 tablespoon lard (or oil)	2 oz. celery, diced
1 tablespoon soya sauce	2 oz. onions, chopped
1 pint stock	1 teaspoon vinegar

1 Boil the noodles for 6 minutes.
2 Rinse under cold water tap and drain.
3 Melt half the lard and fry the noodles for 3 minutes, add soya sauce and stock.
4 Cut all the meat into thin slices.
5 Heat remainder of lard. Fry vegetables in it for 5 minutes.
6 Add meat, fry together for 3 minutes, and serve on top of the braised noodles, sprinkled with vinegar.

Variations

Braised noodles with bamboo shoots and mushrooms
As above, substituting 8 oz. veal, 6 oz. bamboo shoots, sliced, and 4 oz. mushrooms for the lean pork, celery, and onions.

Braised noodles with prawns
As above, substituting 1 pint prawns and 8 oz. broccoli for pork and vegetables.

Braised noodles with lobster and cauliflower
As above, substituting 8 oz. lobster meat, diced, and 8 oz. cauliflower divided into flowerets, for prawns and broccoli.

Pancake rolls

cooking time   25–30 minutes

you will need for 6 servings:

1 tablespoon oil	salt and pepper
6 oz. lean pork, chopped	1 teaspoon sugar
4 oz. onions, chopped	1 dessertspoon soya sauce
4 stalks celery, chopped	2–3 tablespoons stock
2 oz. bamboo shoots, chopped	3 oz. flour
1 leek, chopped	1 oz. cornflour
1 oz. mushrooms, chopped	2 eggs, beaten
4 oz. crab meat, chopped	water
	parsley

1 Heat oil in a pan and fry the pork, onions, celery, bamboo shoots, leek, mushrooms and crab meat for 2 minutes.
2 Season with salt and pepper.
3 Add sugar, soya sauce and stock. Simmer for 8 minutes.
4 Remove and keep until needed.
5 Mix flour, cornflour, a pinch of salt and the eggs in a bowl. Then little by little, add water, stirring all the time until the consistency of a fairly thin batter is reached.
6 Grease a small frying pan while cold, then heat it, pour a little batter into it so that it just covers the bottom and cook on a very low heat for 2 minutes.
7 Turn out the pancake, cooked side up.
8 Put a little of the pork and vegetable mixture in the middle, roll up the pancake, tuck in the ends and seal them with a little beaten egg.
9 Repeat this until all ingredients have been used up.
10 Deep fry the pancake rolls in oil for 3 minutes. Drain, garnish with parsley and serve at once.

Egg rolls

cooking time   25–30 minutes

you will need for 6–8 servings:

Pastry:

8 oz. flour	2 pints water
2 tablespoons cornflour	oil for greasing pan
1 teaspoon salt	1 tablespoon flour mixed
1 egg, beaten	with 2 tablespoons
1 teaspoon sugar	water

1 Sift flour, cornflour and salt into a bowl.
2 Whisk in egg and sugar, add water to make a thin batter.
3 Grease the pan lightly and put over low heat.
4 Whisk the batter and pour a ladleful (3–4 tablespoons) into the middle of the pan, tilting the pan to spread the batter evenly.
5 Pour off any surplus batter, leaving only a thin layer.
6 As soon as the pancake comes away from the edges of the pan, turn it over to cook the other side and remove.
7 When the required number of pancakes has been made, proceed to fill. Remember that both pancakes and filling must be quite cold, otherwise the pastry tends to tear.
8 Fry as described above, drain and serve with a dish of soya sauce or Plum sauce (see under Fan-tail shrimps, page 67).

Filling:

4 oz. celery, minced	2 oz. bamboo shoots, shredded
8 oz. cabbage, finely shredded	4 oz. water chestnuts, thinly sliced
¼ pint boiling water	2–3 spring onions, finely chopped
2 tablespoons oil	
3 oz. cooked shrimps, diced	1 teaspoon salt
3 oz. roast ham (or pork, or any other cooked meat), diced	½ teaspoon pepper
	3 tablespoons soya sauce

1 Cook celery and cabbage in water with a lid on for 2 minutes.
2 Drain and wring out in a cloth to remove all moisture.
3 Heat oil and fry shrimps and meat for 3 minutes, stirring frequently.
4 Add celery, cabbage, bamboo shoots, water chestnuts, spring onions, salt, pepper and soya sauce.
5 Cook gently, stirring all the time, until the mixture acquires a uniform golden colour (2–3 minutes).
6 Leave until cool.
7 Put 3 tablespoons of filling on each pancake, spread the filling lengthwise, fold and roll up as described in the recipe for Pancake rolls using the flour and water mixture for sealing the edges.

Deep fried Chinese patties

cooking time   25–30 minutes

you will need for 4 servings:

1 lb. meat (beef or pork), minced	12 oz. flour
4 oz. onions, chopped	1 egg
4 oz. cabbage, chopped	pinch salt
1 tablespoon soya sauce	½ pint water
1 teaspoon sherry	oil for deep frying

1 Mix the meat, onions and cabbage. Fry in a little oil for 10 minutes.
2 Season with soya sauce and sherry and leave to get cold.
3 Prepare dough using flour, egg, salt and water, adding the latter a little at a time.
4 Mix the dough quickly, roll out wafer thin (always rolling forward), and with a pastry cutter cut out little circles about 3-inches in diameter.
5 Fill with meat.
6 Close the ends tightly, sealing edges with a little cold water.
7 Fry in deep oil until crisp and golden, and serve with soya sauce.

Variations

Semi-fried patties
As above, but instead of deep frying the patties, fry them in 1 oz. oil, browning them on each side. Cover with ¼ pint stock, simmer for 3 minutes, and serve.

Boiled patties
Prepare as above, and drop the patties into a large pan of boiling water. As soon as they float up to the surface, add a few drops of cold water. Drain and serve with soya sauce.

Har Gow (steamed prawn dumplings)

cooking time   20–25 minutes

you will need for 6–8 servings:

1 tablespoon lard	½ teaspoon sesame oil
4 oz. raw pork, minced	pinch salt
2 tablespoons mushrooms, finely chopped	pinch Ve-Tsin
2 spring onions, finely chopped	2 teaspoons light soya sauce
4 Pacific prawns, peeled and chopped	¼ teaspoon sugar
2 tablespoons bamboo shoots, diced	1 tablespoon wine (or sherry)
1 thin slice ginger, finely chopped	½ teaspoon cornflour
	2 tablespoons cold water
	6 oz. Chinese wheat starch (or flour)
	6 oz. boiling water

1 Heat lard in frying pan and toss the pork for 30 seconds.
2 Add mushrooms, spring onions, prawns, bamboo shoots, ginger and sesame oil. 'Scramble' for 30 seconds, season with salt, Ve-Tsin, soya sauce and sugar. Sprinkle in wine.
3 Dilute cornflour in cold water, pour over the contents of the frying pan, stir well and turn out the dumpling filling into a bowl.
4 Mix wheat starch (or flour) with hot water into a stiff dough, adding the water very gradually. Knead well, sprinkle with dry flour and roll into a long sausage.
5 Pinch off small pieces of dough of uniform size, roll out into circles 3-inches in diameter, taking care to fray the edges by scraping them with the lip of a bowl or saucer.
6 Put a good teaspoon of the filling in the middle of each circlet of dough, pinch the edges together to form a semi-circle, steam for 12 minutes and serve piping hot.

Char Shiu Pow (roast pork steamed buns)

cooking time   12–15 minutes

you will need for 8–10 servings:

1 tablespoon peanut oil	1 teaspoon cornflour
4 oz. raw pork, finely chopped	1 teaspoon oyster sauce
1 tablespoon onion, finely chopped	2 tablespoons cold water
	8 oz. plain flour
2 tablespoons mushrooms, finely chopped	½ teaspoon baking powder
pinch salt	1 teaspoon sugar
½ teaspoon soya sauce	½ pint hot water
	vinegar
	soya sauce

1 Heat oil and fry pork quickly, to seal the juices (about 1 minute).
2 Add onion and mushrooms, cook together, stirring constantly, for 1 minute. Season with salt and soya sauce.

3 Mix cornflour with oyster sauce and cold water, blend this mixture into the contents frying pan, cook for a further minute and remove from heat.

4 Mix flour with baking powder and sugar. Add enough water to make a stiff dough. Knead on a floured board until very firm.

5 Divide dough into 8–10 pieces, shape each into a ball, roll out into 2½–3 inch circles.

6 Put a portion of the filling into the middle of each circle. Pinch the edges together.

7 Arrange the 'buns' on a piece of moist cloth on the bottom of a steamer, or place each on a piece of greaseproof paper cut to match, and steam for 10–12 minutes.

8 Serve with vinegar or soya sauce.

Variation

Instead of mushroom, add to the pork spinach (or cabbage), parboiled, drained and finely chopped.

Shao Mai (pork and prawns steamed in pastry)

cooking time   15 minutes

you will need for 6–8 servings:

pastry for noodles (recipe on page 17) using half the quantity	1 tablespoon bamboo shoots, chopped
8 oz. half-lean half-fat pork, minced	pinch salt
	pinch sugar
4 oz. cooled, peeled prawns	pinch Ve-Tsin
1 tablespoon water chestnuts, chopped	1 teaspoon light soya sauce
	pinch grated ginger
	1 tablespoon Chinese wine (or sherry)

1 Prepare the dough, knead well, wrap in a damp cloth and leave until the filling is ready.

2 Put pork in a mixing bowl. Reserve 6–8 prawns for decoration and chop the rest.

3 Combine pork and chopped prawns with the rest of the ingredients, blend well.

4 Break off uniform pieces of dough, roll each piece into a thin circle and fray the edges by scraping with the lip of a bowl or saucer.

5 Put 3 teaspoons filling in the centre of each piece of pastry and pinch the edges to close around the filling, but leave the top free.

6 Garnish the top of each *shao mai* with a whole prawn, stand in a steam cage and steam for 15 minutes. Serve at once.

Shanghai noodles

cooking time   10 minutes

you will need for 6 servings:

1 lb. egg noodles	2½ pints boiling salted water

1 Drop the noodles into the water, cook for 8 minutes and start making your crab sauce (this should take precisely 2 minutes, by which time the noodles will be cooked).

Crab sauce

cooking time   2 minutes

you will need for 6 servings:

2 tablespoons peanut oil	6–8 thin slices ginger
1 large can crab meat	2–3 shallots, sliced
2 tablespoons Chinese wine (or sherry)	salt to taste
	2 tablespoons cornflour
½ pint light stock (or water with a bouillon cube)	¼ pint cold water

1 Heat oil, put in crab meat, stir on fairly high heat for 30 seconds.

2 Add wine, stock, ginger, shallots and salt to taste.

3 Cook, stirring, for 1 minute.

4 Dilute cornflour with cold water, blend into the pan, cook for 30 seconds, stirring constantly.

5 Pour ¼ pint cold water into the pan in which the noodles are cooking, drain at once and arrange the noodles on a heated serving dish.

6 Pour the crab sauce over the noodles and serve.

Velvet noodles

cooking time   10 minutes

you will need for 6 servings:

3 oz. lean pork, cut in thin small slices	1 pint stock (or water with a bouillon cube)
1 oz. fresh mushrooms, sliced	1 cos lettuce, shredded
	1 teaspoon Ve-Tsin
2 teaspoons light soya sauce	salt
	6 oz. rice noodles
1 teaspoon cornflour	2 pints water, salted boiling

1 Sprinkle pork and mushrooms with 1 teaspoon soya sauce as well as the cornflour, mix well.

2 Put in a pan, add stock, bring to the boil and simmer for 8 minutes.

3 Add lettuce, remaining soya sauce and Ve-Tsin.

4 Stir gently and cook for 30 seconds.

5 Taste for seasoning and, if necessary, add salt.

6 Bring noodles to the boil in salted water, simmer for 30 seconds and drain.

7 Arrange on a heated serving dish, pour sauce over the noodles, heaping the pork, mushrooms and lettuce on top, and serve.

Vegetables

Vegetables form an important part of the Chinese diet, and because vegetables, sometimes several vegetables, are eaten daily at every meal, Chinese cooks have evolved countless ways of preparing them. Chinese vegetarian cookery is a highly developed art and such is the ingenuity of these cooks that it would take a separate book, not a mere chapter, to do justice to their skill.

The choice of vegetables in China is vast. Many of these are not available in Europe, others can be found from time to time. I have tried to concentrate mainly on recipes which will teach new ways with old vegetables and on traditional Chinese vegetable recipes.

The Chinese are most particular about the way their vegetables are cooked and served. They must be just right, neither over-cooked nor under-cooked. The principal way of cooking vegetables is semi-frying, which has everything to recommend it. The vegetables, cut up in such a way as to make them look harmonious with the rest of the meal, are quickly tossed in a little lard or oil, which seals their juices and preserves their colour and crispness. A little water, just enough to cover them and induce them to render up their juices, is then added, except in the case of soft vegetables such as lettuce, spinach, and watercress, which need no water at all. Never cook the vegetables under a lid, and use salt as the only seasoning. Soya sauce should not be added to vegetables intended as independent dishes.

Chinese celery salad

no cooking

you will need for 4 servings:

1 head celery	pinch salt
2 pints water, boiling	1 teaspoon sesame oil
1 tablespoon soya sauce	

1 Wash celery stalks, cut into 1½-inch chunks, then slice each chunk into 3–4 pieces lengthwise.
2 Drop celery into boiling water, remove from heat but leave in the water for 2–3 minutes.
3 Drain, rinse with cold water, drain again and chill until required.
4 Combine soya sauce, salt and sesame oil, toss the celery in this dressing and serve.

Chinese asparagus salad

cooking time   3 minutes

you will need for 4–5 servings:

1–1½ lb. asparagus, cut into 1½-inch lengths	1½ tablespoons soya sauce
salt	pinch sugar
1½ pints boiling water.	1 tablespoon salad oil

1 Drop asparagus into salted boiling water. Allow to come up to the boil again.
2 Cook for 3 minutes, drain, rinse with cold water and chill until required.
3 Arrange on a serving dish. Combine soya sauce with sugar and oil, toss the asparagus in this dressing and serve.

Fried spinach

cooking time   5 minutes

you will need for 4 servings:

1 lb. spinach	1 clove garlic, crushed
½ oz. lard (or oil)	1 teaspoon salt

1 Wash the spinach but do not tear off stalks.
2 Heat lard in a pan and fry the spinach quickly. (It will turn a very bright colour as soon as it is put in the hot fat.)
3 Stir to ensure even cooking, allow 2 minutes cooking time, then add garlic and salt.
4 Cook fast together for 3 minutes, stirring all the time, and serve.

Variation

Semi-fried radish tops
Using young radish tops, proceed as descriped above.

Fried cabbage (1)

cooking time   13 minutes

you will need for 4 servings:

½ oz. lard (or oil)	1 teaspoon salt
1 lb. cabbage, cut in ribbons	½ pint water

1 Heat the lard and quick fry the cabbage for 3 minutes, ensuring that every piece is sealed with a film of oil.
2 Add salt and water and cook fast for 10 minutes.

Fried cabbage (2)

cooking time   6 minutes

you will need for 4 servings:

1 lb. cabbage, in fine strips	1 teaspoon vinegar
½ oz. lard (or oil)	1 teaspoon salt
	½ teaspoon sugar

1 Quick fry cabbage in hot fat for 3 minutes.
2 Add vinegar, salt and sugar.
3 Fry for another 3 minutes and serve.

Variations

Fried spring greens
As above, substituting spring greens for cabbage.

Fried Brussels sprouts
As above, substituting Brussels sprouts for spring greens, cutting them in half, if big.

Fried lettuce

cooking time   1–2 minutes

you will need for 4 servings:

1 lettuce	1 teaspoon salt
½ oz. lard (or oil)	1 clove crushed garlic

1 Wash the lettuce thoroughly and break by hand into pieces 2-inches square.
2 Heat oil and quick fry lettuce until leaves turn soft.
3 Season with salt and crushed garlic and serve.

Variation

Fried watercress
As above, allowing 8 oz. watercress in place of lettuce.

Cabbage in milk

cooking time   9–10 minutes

you will need for 4 servings:

1 lb. cabbage	1 teaspoon cornflour
boiling water	¼ pint milk
1 oz. lard (or oil)	salt and pepper
½ pint veal (or chicken stock)	1 oz. finely shredded ham

1 Wash the cabbage, break into pieces 2-inches square, dip into boiling water for 2 minutes and drain.
2 Heat lard and quick fry the cabbage for 2 minutes.

3 Add stock, and cornflour diluted with milk to make a thin paste.
4 Simmer for 5 minutes.
5 Season with salt and pepper and serve garnished with shredded ham.

Cabbage heart with crab sauce

cooking time   12–13 minutes

you will need for 4 servings:

8 oz. cabbage heart	1 teaspoon soya sauce
salt	4 oz. crab meat, flaked
water	(canned or fresh)
1–1½ tablespoons peanut oil	1 teaspoon cornflour
	2 tablespoons cold water
1 clove garlic, crushed	
1 tablespoon Chinese wine (or sherry) (optional)	

1 Cut the cabbage into 1-inch pieces, cook in a little salted boiling water for 7–8 minutes and drain thoroughly.
2 Heat oil in frying pan, add garlic, cook for 2 minutes and discard garlic.
3 Add cabbage, wine and soya sauce. Cook for 1 minute stirring all the time.
4 Add crab meat, stir and cook for 1 minute.
5 Dilute cornflour in cold water, blend into the pan, cook for 1 minute and serve.

Cauliflower, water chestnuts and mushrooms

cooking time   3–4 minutes

you will need for 4 servings:

5 dried mushrooms	¼ pint mushroom water
1 medium-sized cauliflower	2 tablespoons stock
	1 teaspoon sherry
boiling water	2 tablespoons soya sauce
2 tablespoons oil	2 tablespoons cornflour
6 water chestnuts	a few drops of sesame oil

1 Soak the mushrooms in warm water for 20–25 minutes, drain but keep the water.
2 Cut off mushroom stalks, then slice.
3 Divide the cauliflower into flowerets, put into a saucepan, pour on enough boiling water to cover completely.
4 Leave to stand in this water for 5 minutes. Drain well.
5 Heat pan, add oil and fry the mushrooms briskly.
6 Cut each chestnut into quarters and add to mushrooms.
7 Add mushroom water, stock, sherry, soya sauce, cornflour and sesame oil.
8 Simmer for a few seconds, stirring constantly.
9 Add cauliflower, allow it to heat through and serve.

Chinese peas in pods

cooking time   3 minutes

you will need for 4 servings:

1 lb. Chinese peas in pods (or young French beans)	1 teaspoon salt
3 tablespoons oil	¼ pint boiling water

1 Wash the pods and drain thoroughly.
2 Heat oil with salt, stir in pea pods, add boiling water.
3 Stir, cover with a lid and cook for 2 minutes.
4 Stir, cover again and cook for a further minute. Serve.

Note:

Only the tenderest of young peas are suitable for this manner of preparation; the pods of peas which have been allowed to grow to maturity will be too tough.

Foo Yung cauliflower

cooking time   14 minutes

you will need for 4 servings:

1½ lb. cauliflower, divided into flowerets	1 tablespoon cornflour
1 pint water	2 egg whites
salt	1–1½ tablespoons lard
4–6 oz. breast of chicken, minced	2 tablespoons cooked ham, finely shredded

1 Bring cauliflower to the boil in salted water, reduce heat, simmer for 10 minutes and drain.
2 Put chicken into a bowl, season with salt, sprinkle with cornflour, add 2 tablespoons cold water and mix well.
3 Add egg whites and whisk the mixture until light and foamy.
4 Heat lard, add chicken mixture, cook, stirring constantly, for 2 minutes.
5 Add cauliflower, cook together, stirring all the time, for 2 minutes.
6 Put on a heated serving dish, sprinkle the top with ham and serve at once.

Fried beans and celery

cooking time   4 minutes

you will need for 4 servings:

1½ tablespoons oil	2 oz. celery, diced
1 teaspoon salt	½ teaspoon sugar
8 oz. beans, sliced	¼ pint water
1 medium-sized onion, sliced	

1 Heat the oil, add salt.
2 Fry beans and onions quickly for 1 minute.
3 Add celery and fry for 1 minute.
4 Add sugar and water, stir, cook for 2 minutes and serve.

Special mixed vegetables (1)

cooking time   7–8 minutes

you will need for 4 servings:

1 tablespoon oil	2 oz. bamboo shoots, diced
2 tomatoes, crushed and peeled	2 oz. celery, diced
2 oz. onion, diced	2 oz. bean sprouts
2 oz. cabbage, diced	2 oz. chicken (or pork) (optional), finely chopped
2 oz. mushrooms, diced	
2 oz. water chestnuts, diced	1 teaspoon salt

1 Heat the oil, put in the tomatoes, press down with a cooking spoon, adding a little water if necessary to make it yield its juice.
2 Add onion and cabbage, cook for 30 seconds.
3 Add mushrooms, water chestnuts and bamboo shoots, cook for 1 minute.
4 Add celery and cook for 1 minute.
5 Finally, add bean sprouts, as they take less time to cook.
6 Cook for 1 minute, stirring all the time as the various ingredients are added. (If the vegetables look as if they are getting dry, cover with a lid for a few seconds to generate steam.)
7 Add chicken, if this is being used; cook until it turns white, and add salt to taste.

Note:

If meat is used, a teaspoon of soya sauce can be added.

Special mixed vegetables (2)

cooking time   7–8 minutes

you will need for 4 servings:

2 oz. French beans, in 1-inch lengths	2 oz. onion, diced
2 oz. cabbage, diced	2 oz. mushrooms, diced
water	2 oz. broccoli, in 1-inch lengths
1 tablespoon oil	1 teaspoon salt

1 Put French beans and cabbage into fast boiling water for 3 minutes, drain and rinse under cold water tap.
2 Heat the oil.
3 Quick fry onion, cabbage and French beans.
4 Add mushrooms and broccoli, cook for 2 minutes.
5 Season with salt and serve.

Braised marrow

cooking time   10–12 minutes

you will need for 4 servings:

1 lb. marrow	2 tablespoons cold water
1 tablespoon lard (or oil)	4–5 spring onions, finely chopped
1 teaspoon salt	
1 dessertspoon cornflour	

1 Peel and seed the marrow, cut into small cubes and fry until golden.
2 Season with salt, add cornflour diluted with water.
3 Simmer 7–8 minutes.
4 Sprinkle with spring onions, and serve.

Braised carrots

cooking time   10 minutes

you will need for 4 servings:

1 oz. lard (or oil)	salt
1 lb. carrots, scraped and sliced	1 pint water

1 Heat lard and quick fry the carrots for 3 minutes.
2 Season with salt to taste, add water, simmer for 7 minutes and serve.

Sweet and sour carrots

cooking time   7–8 minutes

you will need for 4 servings:

1 lb. new carrots	1½ tablespoons vinegar
1 tablespoon peanut oil	1½ tablespoons sugar
pinch salt	1 teaspoon cornflour
½ pint water	

1 Brush and rinse the carrots, cut into slanting slices. Fry in oil for 1 minute.
2 Season with salt, add half the water, cook for 4–5 minutes.
3 Combine remaining ingredients with the rest of the water, stir into the pan, cook for 2 minutes, stirring constantly and serve.

Braised broad beans

cooking time   12–15 minutes

you will need for 4 servings:

1 tablespoon oil	water
1 teaspoon salt	1 tablespoon spring
1 lb. broad beans, shelled	onions, chopped

1 Heat the oil, add salt and quick fry the beans for 1 minute.
2 Add enough water to cover and simmer for 12–15 minutes.
3 Sprinkle with spring onions and serve.

Variation

Braised peas
As above, substituting peas for broad beans, and reducing the cooking time to 5 minutes.

Braised turnips

cooking time   8 minutes

you will need for 4 servings:

1 lb. turnips, peeled and grated	½ pint water
1 oz. lard (or oil)	few spring onions, chopped
salt and pepper	

1 Quick fry the turnips for 3 minutes, season with salt and pepper to taste.
2 Add water, simmer for 5 minutes, sprinkle with spring onions and serve.

Pickled turnips

cooking time   5 minutes

you will need for 4 servings:

8 oz. turnips, peeled and sliced	1 tablespoon lard (or oil)
1 tablespoon salt	1 tablespoon vinegar
	1 tablespoon sesame oil

1 Sprinkle turnips with salt and leave to stand for 8–12 hours. (Do not become alarmed if they become discoloured. This will be rectified during cooking.)
2 Quickly fry in hot lard for 5 minutes.
3 Add vinegar, stir, remove from heat.
4 Sprinkle with sesame oil and serve, either hot as a vegetable, or cold as a salad.

Turnip tops

cooking time   3 minutes

you will need for 4 servings:

1 lb. turnip tops, washed	1 oz. lard (or oil)
boiling water	1 teaspoon salt

1 Put turnip tops in a colander and pour boiling water to soften them.
2 Shred and quick fry for 3 minutes.
3 Add salt and serve.

Braised bean sprouts (1)

cooking time   3 minutes

you will need for 4 servings:

1 lb. bean sprouts	½ teaspoon vinegar
1 oz. lard (or oil)	salt

1 Soak bean sprouts in water and rinse them under a cold water tap until all the skins have been washed away.
2 Drain in a towel and quick fry in lard for 3 minutes.
3 Add vinegar, season with salt to taste, and serve.

Braised bean sprouts (2)

cooking time   3½ minutes

you will need for 4 servings:

1 lb. bean sprouts	pinch sugar
1 tablespoon oil	1 teaspoon soya sauce
1 teaspoon salt	2 tablespoons water

1 Wash and drain the bean sprouts as in recipe for Braised bean sprouts (1).
2 Quick fry in oil with salt for 30 seconds, stirring all the time.
3 Add sugar, soya sauce and water.
4 Stir, cook for 3 minutes and serve.

Fried bean sprouts

cooking time   4 minutes

you will need for 4 servings:

1½ lb. bean sprouts	1 teaspoon cornflour
1 tablespoon beef (or pork) dripping	2 tablespoons water
½ pint stock	1 teaspoon sesame oil
1 oz. spring onions	1 teaspoon soya sauce

1 Wash and drain bean sprouts as in recipe for Braised bean sprouts (1).
2 Quick fry in dripping for 30 seconds.
3 Add stock and simmer for 3 minutes.
4 Add spring onions cut into pieces 1½-inches long, cornflour diluted with the water, sesame oil and soya sauce.
5 Cook for 30 seconds and serve.

Fried bean sprouts with tomatoes

cooking time   5 minutes

you will need for 4 servings:

1 lb. bean sprouts	1 teaspoon cornflour
1 tablespoon lard (or oil)	2 tablespoons water
salt	1 teaspoon sesame oil
stock to cover	pepper
8 oz. tomatoes, skinned	spring onions

1 Wash and drain bean sprouts as in recipe for Braised bean sprouts (1).
2 Heat oil in pan, add salt to taste.
3 Quick fry the bean sprouts for 1 minute, stirring constantly.
4 Add stock and simmer for 2 minutes.
5 Add tomatoes and cook for 1 minute.
6 Pour in cornflour diluted with water.
7 Add sesame oil, pepper to taste, and the spring onions cut into pieces 1½-inches long.
8 Cook for 1 minute and serve.

Silver sprouts with pork

cooking time   9–10 minutes

you will need for 4 servings:

8 oz. lean, white pork	1 tablespoon lard
6 oz. bean sprouts	1 oz. chives, cut in 1-inch lengths
pinch salt	
1 teaspoon cornflour	2–3 tablespoons stock
1 teaspoon light coloured soya sauce	

1 Cut the pork into very thin slices.
2 Wash and drain bean sprouts thoroughly.
3 Season pork with salt and sprinkle with cornflour and soya sauce.
4 Heat lard and quick fry the bean sprouts for 2 minutes. Remove. In the same fat fry the pork, stirring constantly, for 5 minutes.
5 Add bean sprouts and chives, check seasoning.
6 Add stock, cook for 2 minutes and serve.

Fried watercress with bean curd

cooking time   3½ minutes

you will need for 4 servings:

1 lb. watercress	½ teaspoon sugar
2 tablespoons lard (or oil)	2 pieces white bean curd
1 teaspoon salt	2 tablespoons water

1 Wash the watercress, drain on a cloth, and chop into 1-inch pieces.
2 Heat lard, add salt, and quickly toss the watercress for 30 seconds, stirring all the time.
3 Add sugar and bean curd diluted with water.
4 Blend in, add the water, simmer for 3 minutes and serve.

Spinach with bean curd

cooking time   3½ minutes

you will need for 4 servings:

1 lb. spinach	2 pieces white bean curd
2 tablespoons lard (or oil)	3 tablespoons water
1 teaspoon salt	½ teaspoon sugar

1 Wash the spinach.
2 Heat lard in pan, add salt and spinach.
3 Semi-fry quickly for about 30 seconds, stirring all the time.
4 Dilute the bean curd with 1 tablespoon water and add to the pan, together with the sugar and rest of water.
5 Blend well, cook for 3 minutes and serve.

Fried mixed vegetables

cooking time   8 minutes

you will need for 4 servings:

1 tablespoon oil	4 oz. leeks, in fine strips
4 oz. turnips, in fine strips	1 teaspoon salt
4 oz. carrots, in fine strips	few drops vinegar
4 oz. celery, in fine strips	1 teaspoon sesame oil

1 Heat the oil and fry all vegetables together quickly for 5 minutes.
2 Add salt and vinegar and continue quick frying for 3 minutes.
3 Remove from heat and allow to cool.
4 Serve as a salad, dressed with sesame oil.

Braised Chinese cabbage

cooking time $3\frac{1}{2}$ minutes

you will need for 4 servings:

8 oz. bundle Chinese cabbage (or ordinary cabbage)	1 teaspoon salt
	pinch sugar
$1\frac{1}{2}$ tablespoons lard (or oil)	1 teaspoon soya sauce
	2 tablespoons water

1 Wash and cut the cabbage in 1-inch pieces.
2 Heat lard and quick fry the cabbage with salt for 20–30 seconds, stirring all the time.
3 Add sugar, soya sauce and water. Blend.
4 Cook for 3 minutes and serve.

Variations

Braised cauliflower
As above, substituting a medium-sized cauliflower divided into flowerets, for the cabbage.

Braised cauliflower and pea pods
As above, allowing a medium-sized cauliflower divided into flowerets, and 4 oz. young peas, using pods and all. See note in recipe for Chinese peas in pods (page 84).

Braised pimentos
As above, substituting 1 lb. cored and seeded pimentos for the cauliflower.

Stuffed pimentos

cooking time   25–30 minutes

you will need for 4 servings:

1 lb. green pimentos	1 clove garlic, crushed
1 lb. lean pork	1 teaspoon soya sauce
1 dessertspoon black soya beans	1 dessertspoon brandy
	salt

1 Wash, core and seed the pimentos and mince the pork.
2 Pour boiling water on the beans, drain and crush them with a spoon.
3 Add garlic, soya sauce and brandy, mix with pork and season with salt.
4 Stir the mixture to ensure smoothness and stuff the pimentos with it.
5 Place in a slightly greased dish and steam for 25–30 minutes.

Variation

Stuffed bitter melon
As above, substituting 1 lb. bitter melons (or cucumber and green pepper), cored and seeded, for pimentos.

Bitter melon with pork ribs

cooking time   40 minutes

you will need for 4 servings:

1 lb. spare pork ribs	1 tablespoon black soya beans
4 bitter melons (or cucumbers and green peppers)	1 tablespoon lard or oil
	2 cloves garlic, crushed
1 dessertspoon soya sauce	salt
1 dessertspoon brandy	$\frac{3}{4}$ pint water
boiling water	$\frac{1}{2}$ teaspoon cornflour

1 Cut the pork into thin pieces, bones and all, 1-inch by $\frac{1}{2}$-inch.
2 Cut the melons in halves, remove seeds and cut into $\frac{1}{4}$-inch slices.
3 Sprinkle the pork with soya sauce and brandy.
4 Pour boiling water on the soya beans, drain and crush them with a fork.
5 Heat oil with garlic, remove garlic when it browns.
6 Put in pork, season with salt to taste and quick fry.
7 As soon as the pork turns white, add soya beans and cook, stirring constantly for 5 minutes.
8 Add water, simmer gently for 20 minutes, add melon, mix, cover and simmer for 10 minutes.
9 Dilute cornflour with water, add to the pan, stir to thicken the sauce and serve.

Variation

Pimentos with pork ribs
As above, substituting 1 lb. of cored, seeded pimentos for the bitter melon (or cucumber and green pepper).

Bamboo shoots and mushrooms

cooking time   5 minutes

you will need for 4 servings:

12 diced mushrooms, soaked and cut into strips	4 tablespoons soya sauce
	1 tablespoon sherry
	1 tablespoon sugar
8 oz. bamboo shoots, sliced	2 tablespoons mushroom water
8 tablespoons oil	1 tablespoon cornflour

1 Soak mushrooms for 20 minutes in warm water to cover.
2 Toss bamboo shoots in 6 tablespoons oil for a few seconds. Drain.
3 Fry mushrooms in 2 tablespoons oil.
4 Add soya sauce, sherry and sugar. Blend.
5 Add bamboo shoots and mushroom water mixed with cornflour.
6 Simmer gently for 2–3 minutes, stirring slowly, and serve.

Bamboo shoots with soya sauce

cooking time   6–7 minutes

you will need for 6 servings:

8 oz. bamboo shoots, sliced	3 tablespoons sugar
oil for deep frying	1 tablespoon cornflour
5 tablespoons soya sauce	¼ pint water

1 Deep fry the bamboo shoots lightly and drain.
2 Reheat in a shallow pan, add soya sauce and mix well.
3 Add a mixture of sugar, cornflour and water.
4 Blend in, simmer for 3 minutes and serve.

Braised broccoli

cooking time   4–5 minutes

you will need for 4 servings:

1 lb. broccoli	1 pinch sugar
1½ tablespoons oil	1 teaspoon soya sauce
1 teaspoon salt	4 tablespoons water

1 Wash, dry and cut the broccoli into 1-inch pieces.
2 Quick fry it in oil with salt for 20 seconds, stirring all the time.
3 Add sugar, soya sauce and water, mix well, simmer for 3–4 minutes and serve.

Variation
Braised asparagus

cooking time   7–8 minutes

As above, substituting 1 lb. asparagus cut into 1-inch chunks for the broccoli.

Asparagus tips

cooking time   4–5 minutes

you will need for 4 servings:

2 tablespoons oil	2 tablespoons soya sauce
2 tablespoons chicken stock	1 tablespoon cornflour
2 tablespoons water	1 lb. asparagus tips, cooked
1 tablespoon sherry	

1 Heat pan, add oil, stock, water, sherry, soya sauce and cornflour, stirring constantly until the mixture boils.
2 Drain the cooked asparagus tips (canned asparagus can be used).
3 Add to the pan, heat thoroughly and serve.

Variations
Chinese peas (or young French beans)

cooking time   2 minutes

As above, substituting Chinese peas (or young French beans), but do not cook for more than 2 minutes.

Courgettes

cooking time   3–4 minutes

As above, substituting courgettes for Chinese peas.

Cucumber

cooking time   2–3 minutes

As above, substituting cucumbers, cut in quarters and then into 1-inch chunks, for the courgettes.

Chinese pickled cucumber (1)

no cooking

you will need for 4 servings:

1 good-sized cucumber	1 clove garlic, crushed
2 tablespoons vinegar	1 teaspoon sesame oil
½ teaspoon salt	

1 Cut the cucumber into thin slices, put in a bowl.
2 Sprinkle with vinegar, salt, garlic and – at the last minute – sesame oil.

Note:

If it has enough moisture this cucumber will keep for several days.

Chinese pickled cucumber (2)

no cooking

you will need for 4 servings:

1 good-sized cucumber
3 tablespoons vinegar
2 tablespoons sugar

1 teaspoon green ginger,
   finely pounded

1 Partly peel the cucumber, i.e. leaving on alternate strips of peel, and slice it very thinly.
2 Bring vinegar, sugar and ginger to the boil in a saucepan.
3 Pour over the cucumber, allow to cool and serve.

Pickled radishes

no cooking

you will need for 4 servings:

2 bundles radishes
1 tablespoon soya sauce
1 tablespoon vinegar

pinch salt
pinch sugar
1 dessertspoon sesame oil

1 Wash, top and tail the radishes.
2 Make a criss-cross cut on top to make them open out.
3 Sprinkle with soya sauce, vinegar, salt, sugar and sesame oil.
4 Serve as a salad.

Pickled celery

no cooking

you will need for 4 servings:

1 large head celery
1 teaspoon salt
1 tablespoon vinegar

1 tablespoon soya sauce
1 dessertspoon sesame oil

1 Wash the celery, remove all stringy bits, cut into thick chunks, put in a colander and scald with boiling water.
2 Drain and dry.
3 Season with salt, vinegar, soya sauce and sesame oil, adding all these condiments while the celery is still hot.
4 Serve hot or cold.

Pickled cabbage

cooking time   3 minutes

you will need for 4 servings:

1 medium-sized white
   cabbage
1 oz. oil
1 dessertspoon soya sauce

1 tablespoon vinegar
1 teaspoon sesame oil
½ teaspoon garlic,
   crushed

1 Wash the cabbage and break into pieces 2-inches square.

2 Heat the oil and quick fry cabbage for 3 minutes.
3 Put in a bowl, add soya sauce, vinegar, sesame oil and garlic.
4 Mix well and serve as a salad.

Note:

Cabbage prepared in this way will keep for several days but must be stirred each day.

Mushrooms in gravy

cooking time   2 hours 15 minutes

you will need for 4 servings:

¼ oz. garlic, crushed
2 tablespoons oil
4 oz. thick dried
   mushrooms
¼ oz. ginger, crushed
stock
1 teaspoon pork dripping

1 pinch sugar
1 teaspoon soya sauce
salt
1 teaspoon cornflour
2 tablespoons cold water
few drops sesame oil

1 Cook garlic in a hot oiled pan for 1 minute and remove.
2 Put in mushrooms and cook for 5–6 minutes.
3 Transfer mushrooms to saucepan, add ginger and double the amount of stock required to cover them.
4 Bring to boil, then simmer gently for 2 hours.
5 Take out and throw away the ginger.
6 Strain the mushrooms, keeping the stock, arrange mushrooms in a dish.
7 Bring mushroom stock to the boil, add dripping, sugar, soya sauce and salt to taste.
8 Cook for 1 minute, add cornflour diluted with water and sesame oil.
9 Cook for 1 minute, pour over the mushrooms and serve.

Boiled mushrooms

cooking time   2 hours 10 minutes

you will need for 4 servings:

1 tablespoon oil
1 small piece garlic,
   crushed
4 oz. thick dried
   mushrooms

2 oz. ginger, crushed
stock
salt
few drops sesame oil

1 Heat oil with garlic.
2 Cook garlic until it browns, then take it out of the pan, and cook the mushrooms in the same oil for 5 minutes.
3 Put mushrooms in a saucepan with ginger and double the amount of stock required to cover them. Simmer gently for 2 hours.
4 Remove ginger, add salt to taste, and sesame oil and serve.

Mushrooms with quenelles

cooking time　　　　　　　2 hours 15 minutes

you will need for 4 servings:

3 oz. water chestnuts,　　2 tablespoons oil
　crushed　　　　　　　1 clove garlic, crushed
6 oz. pork, minced　　　3 oz. thick dried
1 teaspoon salt　　　　　　mushrooms
1 oz. cornflour　　　　　2 oz. fresh ginger

1 Mix chestnuts with pork, season with salt and chop together to achieve a smooth mixture.
2 Shape into small balls, roll them in cornflour.
3 Heat the oil with garlic until garlic browns, then take it out.
4 Put mushrooms in some oil and cook for 10 minutes.
5 Transfer mushrooms to a saucepan, add ginger and double the amount of stock required to cover.
6 Simmer gently for 2 hours.
7 Poach the quenelles (meat balls) in stock for 20 minutes.
8 Drain them and put on a serving dish.
9 Remove ginger from mushrooms.
10 Put the mushrooms on top of quenelles and serve.

Fresh mushrooms with mixed vegetables

cooking time　　　　　　　25 minutes

you will need for 4 servings:

2 pieces white bean curd　1 oz. lily petals
2 tablespoons oil　　　　3 oz. spinach
½ oz. corn noodles　　　½ teaspoon sugar
4 oz. mushrooms　　　　1 teaspoon cornflour
stock　　　　　　　　　2 tablespoons cold water
salt　　　　　　　　　　sesame oil

1 Put the bean curd into boiling oil and cook for 3 minutes.
2 Remove and cut into fine slices.
3 Immerse corn noodles in boiling oil for 4 minutes.
4 Put mushrooms in an oiled pan, add double the amount of stock required to cover them.
5 Cook for 5 minutes and add salt to taste.
6 Add lily petals, bean curd, corn noodles and spinach and cook for 5 minutes.
7 Sprinkle with sugar and cook for 4 minutes.
8 Dilute cornflour with water, pour in to the pan, blend.
9 Sprinkle with sesame oil, cook for 1 minute and serve.

Bean curd

cooking time　　　　　　　3–4 minutes

you will need for 4 servings:

1 lb. bean curd　　　　　1 teaspoon cornflour
2 oz. lard (or oil)　　　2 tablespoons cold water
4 oz. fresh mushrooms　　1 dessertspoon soya sauce
few spring onions,
　chopped

1 Cut bean curd into oblong pieces and put into boiling lard to brown both sides.
2 Add mushrooms and spring onions.
3 Stir gently to avoid breaking up the bean curd.
4 Add cornflour diluted with water.
5 Season with soya sauce and serve.

Mushrooms with peas in oyster sauce

cooking time　　　　　　　10 minutes

you will need for 4 servings:

8 oz. fresh mushrooms　　½ pint chicken stock (or
1 packet frozen peas　　　　water with a bouillon
salted water　　　　　　　cube)
1–2 tablespoons peanut　　1 teaspoon soya sauce
　oil　　　　　　　　　1 teaspoon cornflour
½ oz. spring onions,　　　pinch Ve-Tsin
　chopped　　　　　　　2 oz. oyster sauce
½ oz. fresh ginger,　　　a few drops sesame oil
　thinly sliced

1 Wash the mushrooms quickly without soaking and dry on cloth.
2 Cook the peas in 2–3 tablespoons lightly salted water for 2 minutes and drain.
3 Heat oil and fry spring onions and ginger for 1 minute. Add mushrooms, peas, stock and soya sauce.
4 Sprinkle in cornflour and Ve-Tsin, stir to blend well and cook for 5 minutes.
5 Blend in oyster sauce, cook for 2 minutes.
6 Sprinkle with sesame oil and serve.

Stuffed mushrooms

cooking time　　　　　　　12–14 minutes

you will need for 4 servings:

8 fresh mushrooms,　　　2 tablespoons soya sauce
　(1½-inch in diameter)　pinch salt
8 oz. pork, minced　　　1 tablespoon sherry
2 water chestnuts, finely　2 tablespoons cornflour
　chopped　　　　　　3–4 spring onions, cut
2–3 slices bamboo shoots,　　in 1½-inch lengths
　finely chopped　　　½ teaspoon sugar

1 Wash the mushroom caps quickly, without soaking, and drain.
2 Remove but keep stems. Combine pork with water chestnuts, bamboo shoots, 1 tablespoon soya sauce, salt, sherry and 1 tablespoon cornflour.
3 Blend the stuffing well.
4 Fill the mushroom caps with the stuffing, piling it into a firm dome. Using about 1 pint boiling water in the bottom part of a steamer, steam the mushrooms for 10–12 minutes.
5 Remove carefully and arrange on a heated serving dish.
6 Slice mushroom stems, and put with remaining soya sauce and cornflour and sugar into a small saucepan, gradually dilute with ½ pint of water over which the mushrooms were steamed.
7 Boil rapidly for 2 minutes to thicken the sauce, pour over mushrooms and serve.
8 Garnish with spring onions.

Bean curd with oyster sauce

cooking time   3–4 minutes

you will need for 4 servings:

1 lb. bean curd	3 tablespoons oyster
4 oz. fresh mushrooms,	sauce
3 tablespoons peanut oil	pepper

1 Cut the bean curd into oblong pieces.
2 Quick fry the mushrooms in peanut oil and put aside.
3 Brown bean curd pieces on both sides, shaking the pan from time to time and basting them with oil. (Avoid stirring as the curd is very fragile.)
4 Pour oyster sauce over the bean curd slices, reduce heat and sauté long enough to impregnate with the sauce.
5 Add mushrooms, reheat, season with pepper and serve.

Bean curd with fresh shrimps

cooking time   3 minutes

you will need for 4 servings:

8 oz. bean curd	4 oz. shelled peas
3–4 tablespoons peanut oil	2 oz. fresh mushrooms, sliced
4 oz. fresh shrimps, peeled and diced	1 tablespoon sherry
few spring onions, chopped	1 dessertspoon soya sauce
	½ teapoon salt
	½ teaspoon pepper

1 Cut the bean curd into oblong pieces, put them in a frying basket.
2 Dip into boiling water for 10 seconds. Drain.
3 Heat oil to boiling point, throw in the diced shrimps, cook for 10 seconds.
4 Add bean curd and spring onions. Cook together for 1 minute.
5 Add peas and mushrooms. Cook for 1 minute.
6 Add sherry, soya sauce, salt and pepper. Turn off heat. Stir gently and serve.

Bean curd and ham fritters

cooking time   1 hour 10 minutes

you will need for 4 servings:

8 oz. bean curd	4 oz. ham, sliced
pork and chicken stock	flour
1 dessertspoon soya sauce	2 eggs, beaten
½ teaspoon powdered ginger	oil for deep frying

1 Cut bean curd into square pieces about 1-inch in size and about ¼-inch thick.
2 Put them in a frying basket and dip into boiling water for 30 seconds. Drain.
3 Put into a saucepan, with enough stock to cover, season with soya sauce and ginger and simmer gently for 1 hour.
4 Place a similarly sized piece of ham on each piece of bean curd. Dredge with flour.
5 Dip in egg and deep fry until golden.
6 Drain and serve.

Stuffed bean curd fritters

cooking time   7–8 minutes

you will need for 4 servings:

8 oz. bean curd	1 dessertspoon soya sauce
2 oz. fresh fish	salt and pepper
2 oz. fresh shrimps, minced	1 tablespoon roasted peanuts, chopped
½ oz. spring onions, chopped	oil for deep frying

1 Cut bean curd into triangular pieces.
2 Make a fairly large hole in the cut side.
3 Pound the fish, mix with shrimps, add spring onions, soya sauce, salt and pepper and roasted peanuts.
4 Blend this forcemeat and use it for stuffing the bean curd triangles.
5 Deep fry in oil until golden, drain and serve.

Bean curd with fish

cooking time   25 minutes

you will need for 4 servings:

8 oz. bean curd	1 dessertspoon soya sauce
2 tablespoons peanut oil	1 oz. spring onions,
8 oz. fresh fish (any	chopped
fish of suitable size)	salt and pepper
1 tablespoon sherry	½ pint water
1 teaspoon green ginger,	
minced	

1 Cut bean curd into oblong pieces.
2 Heat peanut oil and fry the fish whole.
3 When fish is golden on both sides, pour the sherry mixed with green ginger over it, add soya sauce, spring onions, salt and pepper to taste and water. (The water can be poured in little by little as it becomes absorbed.)
4 Simmer the fish for 15 minutes, add bean curd and cook together for 5 minutes, then serve.

Stuffed cucumber halves

cooking time   55 minutes

you will need for 6 servings:

2 oz. dried mushrooms,	3 tablespoons onion,
chopped	chopped
1 lb. pork (or veal or	1 tablespoon fresh
chicken, minced)	ginger, chopped
3 tablespoons oil	6 cucumbers (each about
½ teaspoon salt	6 inches long)
3 tablespoons soya sauce	½ pint stock
3 tablespoons cornflour	½ pint water

1 Soak mushrooms in warm water for 20 minutes.
2 Mix pork with 1 tablespoon oil, salt, 1 tablespoon soya sauce, 1 tablespoon cornflour, onions and mushrooms.
3 Add ginger and blend well.
4 Peel the cucumbers in strips, lengthwise, leaving alternate strips of unpeeled skin (this helps to preserve the shape of the vegetable).
5 Cut in half lengthwise, then into 2-inch pieces across.
6 Scoop out seeds and refill with the meat mixture.
7 Pour 2 tablespoons oil into a large pan, arrange stuffed cucumbers in this and add stock.
8 Cover with a well fitting lid, cook on moderate heat for 12 minutes, then reduce heat and simmer gently for 35–40 minutes.
9 Carefully remove cucumber from pan and keep hot.
10 In the same pan blend the remaining 2 tablespoons cornflour, 2 tablespoons soya sauce and ½ pint water.
11 Cook for a few minutes until the sauce thickens, pour over the cucumbers and serve at once.

Broccoli Hong Kong style

cooking time   10 minutes

you will need for 4 servings:

1 lb. broccoli	1 teaspoon gin
3 tablespoons oil	1 teaspoon sugar
1 teaspoon salt	2 tablespoons stock (or
2 tablespoons soya sauce	water)

1 Wash the broccoli and cut into pieces 1½-inches long.
2 Heat oil, sprinkle in salt, and cook the broccoli uncovered for 8 minutes, shaking the pan from time to time.
3 Mix soya sauce, gin and sugar and pour over the broccoli.
4 Add hot stock, cover, bring to the boil, cook for 2 minutes and serve.

Aubergines, Cantonese style

cooking time   15 minutes

you will need for 6 servings:

1½ lb. aubergines	4 pimentos, seeded and
boiling water	diced
8 oz. chicken (or veal),	1 clove garlic, finely
uncooked	chopped
1 tablespoon cornflour	1 tablespoon fresh
2 tablespoons soya sauce	ginger, finely pounded
1 tablespoon brandy	¼ pint chicken stock
4 tablespoons oil	

1 Cut the aubergines into shoe string strips, cover with boiling water, allow to stand for 5 minutes and drain.
2 Cut the chicken meat (breast preferably) into similar thin, long strips.
3 Mix cornflour, soya sauce and brandy and coat the chicken with this mixture.
4 Heat oil in pan. Fry pimentos until they change colour.
5 Remove and in the same pan fry the chicken, 3–4 minutes.
6 Add aubergines, garlic, pimentos, ginger and stock.
7 Cook for one minute and serve.

Lettuce with dried shrimps

cooking time   3½ minutes

you will need for 4 servings:

1 tablespoon dried	2 tablespoons oil
shrimps	1 teaspoon salt
2 tablespoons hot water	½ teaspoon sugar
1 lb. cos lettuce	1 teaspoon soya sauce

1 Wash shrimps and soak in hot water for 30 minutes.
2 Clean the lettuce and break into pieces 2-inches square.
3 Heat oil. Add salt and lettuce and quick fry for 10–15 seconds, stirring all the time.
4 Add sugar, soya sauce, shrimps and their water. Mix.
5 Cook for 3 minutes and serve.

Variation:

Cabbage with dried shrimps
As above, substituting cabbage for lettuce.

Beef flavoured bean sprouts

cooking time   6–7 minutes
you will need for 4 servings:

8 oz. beef, shredded	2 tablespoons soya sauce
4 tablespoons cooking oil	¼ pint stock (or water)
1 sliver garlic	3 teaspoons cornflour
2 teaspoons salt	4 tablespoons cold water
½ teaspoon green ginger, crushed	3–4 spring onions, cut in 1-inch pieces
1 lb. bean sprouts	

1 Cook the beef for 2 minutes in hot oil, with garlic, salt and ginger.
2 In the same pan toss bean sprouts, add soya sauce and stock, bring to the boil and simmer gently for 3 minutes.
3 Add cornflour mixed with water to sauce, sprinkle with spring onions and serve.

String beans with bean curd

cooking time   5–6 minutes
you will need for 4 servings:

4 tablespoons oil	1 lb. string beans
3 cubes or tablespoons bean curd	generous ¼ pint hot water

1 Heat oil in a pan, add bean curd and stir well to mash the curd thoroughly.
2 Add beans, mix until the curd is melted, add water, stir.
3 Bring to boiling point, reduce heat, cover with a lid and simmer for 2 minutes.
4 Stir, cover and cook for further 3–4 minutes, depending on how well done you like your beans. Serve at once.

Chicken flavoured chestnuts

cooking time   40–45 minutes
you will need for 6–8 servings:

30 chestnuts	4 tablespoons soya sauce
6 dried mushrooms	1 teaspoon salt
8 oz. chicken meat uncooked	1 tablespoon sugar
2 tablespoons oil	1 tablespoon sherry
1 medium-sized onion, chopped	1 tablespoon cornflour
1 tablespoon fresh ginger, chopped	1 pint hot chicken stock (or water)

1 Boil the chestnuts for 30 minutes and peel.
2 Soak the mushrooms in enough warm water to cover for 30 minutes, drain, cut off stalks and slice mushrooms into thin strips.
3 Cut chicken meat into 1-inch pieces.
4 Heat 1 tablespoon oil in pan, fry the onion until golden and remove.
5 Reheat pan, add another tablespoon oil and brown the chicken quickly with the ginger.
6 Add mushrooms and cook together for one minute.
7 Mix soya sauce, salt, sugar, sherry and cornflour, add to chicken and stir for one minute.
8 Add onions, hot stock and chestnuts.
9 Simmer until the chicken is tender and serve very hot.

Spinach and mushrooms

cooking time   2 hours
you will need for 4 servings:

14 dried mushrooms, sliced	1 tablespoon sugar
½ pint warm water	½ teaspoon salt
3 tablespoons oil	1 tablespoon cornflour
4 tablespoons soya sauce	1 tablespoon water
1 tablespoon sherry	1 lb. spinach (or one large frozen packet)

1 Soak the mushrooms in ½ pint warm water for 20 minutes, drain but keep the water.
2 Cut off mushroom stalks. Heat pan, add oil and fry the mushrooms until golden.
3 Add soya sauce, sherry, sugar and salt and cook for ¼ minute.
4 Add mushroom water and simmer for 2 hours.
5 Add cornflour mixed with water, cook until sauce thickens.
6 Wash the spinach and shake off all moisture from the leaves.
7 Put in a saucepan over low heat, *without adding any water*. Heat the spinach through, turning the leaves over.
8 Keep on low heat long enough to warm all the spinach thoroughly, put on a serving dish.
9 Top with mushrooms and sauce and serve.

A Note on Tea

The significance of tea in the Chinese social life must not be overlooked. It is the symbol of welcome with which one is greeted on arrival in a Chinese home and is responsible for the Chinese reputation of the soberest of all nations.

A tea plant cannot be transplanted—it was therefore considered symbolic of faithfulness and used to play an important part among the presents given for an engagement. 'Accepting tea' used to be synonymous with 'becoming engaged' and spilling the tea was considered a bad omen.

Tea, in use since the Tang dynasty (A.D. 618–906) is grown all over China and, broadly speaking, although there are many varieties, there are two categories of China tea: Green, and black which had always been called 'red' in China. Both green and black tea come from the same plant—the difference arises out of the different methods of drying the leaves.

As with many other good things that grow on this lovely planet, the younger the leaves when cropped, the better the tea. Some green teas in China were labelled 'Before the rain', to indicate that the leaves were picked before the rainfall could stimulate their growth and make them that much coarser.

The best known red teas in the West are *Lapsang Souchong* and *Oolung*. Most teas sold in shops are blends either of different varieties of tea leaves, or of tea leaves and some other leaves, such as jasmine, lichi, chrysanthemum, camelia, rose and many others, but the quality will inevitably depend on the grade of the tea used in the mixture.

The best green tea which enjoys popularity in China as well as in the West, is *Lung Jiing* (Dragon's Well).

The Chinese, whatever their social position, drink tea at all meals and at all times. And, to do the tea justice, they drink it without milk or sugar.

Good tea should never be hoarded or bought in large quantities, it does not get any better in 'maturing'. Tea is extremely sensitive and can easily be affected by contact with other things—therefore, always keep it separately to protect the flavour and aroma.

To make China tea, for best results, use a porcelain or earthenware (never a metal) tea pot and rinse it thoroughly with boiling water. Allow a level teaspoon for every guest —but none for the pot!

Make sure the water in your kettle is fresh and freshly boiled. As soon as it bubbles, pour it over the tea leaves in the pot, stir once with a clean spoon, leave to stand for three minutes and serve. For people who prefer their tea weak, dilute by pouring hot water direct into their cups, not into the tea pot.

When serving a specially good tea, use very small, 'liqueur-size' cups and heat them by rinsing with boiling water, before pouring out the precious liquid.

All China tea retains both its flavour and wholesomeness for 10–12 hours after making and can safely be strained and reheated.

Index